UTES

The Mountain People

◆◆◆

REVISED EDITION

JAN PETTIT

Introduction by Eddie Box

Johnson Books: Boulder

Dedicated to my beautiful daughters,
Kim, Lin, and Jil,
and all other natives of the mountains

"If I had read more widely I should never have completed this book. If I had even known how much there was to read, I would never have dared to start to write it all."

H.M. and N.K. Chadwick
Growth of English Literature

© 1990 by Jan Pettit

Seventh Printing 2003

ISBN 1-55566-065-7

LCCCN 90-91905

Cover design by Molly Gough

Cover: War Chief Buckskin Charlie (Charles Buck) spent his youth learning warrior skills, hunting, providing for his family, and fighting his enemies. As a young man he sat by Chief Ouray's side during treaty negotiations in Colorado and Washington, D.C. As he watched his lifestyle slip away he became a strong, determined yet fair leader of the Southern Ute people. He is wearing a scalp shirt fringed with horse hair and an 1890 Benjamin Harrison peace medal—the last medal designed specifically for presentation to Indians. Cover drawing by Molly Gough from a Lisle Updyke Photo, courtesy of Dr. Robert W. Delaney.

Printed in the United States of America by
Johnson Printing Company
1880 South 57th Court
Boulder, Colorado 80301

Contents

Acknowledgments

There have been volumes written for serious students concerning the Ute people. Several scholars have devoting their lives to this subject. Robert W. Delaney (Fort Lewis College), Kathryn L. MacKay, Floyd A. O'Neil, and Gregory C. Thompson (University of Utah), Gottfried Lang, and Omer Stewart (University of Colorado) are a few of those dedicated scholars who were willing to share their valuable time to guide me.

Clifford Duncan, Museum Director, Uintah-Ouray Reservation; Eddie Box; Isabell and Cynthia Kent; Bertha Grove; Everett Burch; and the Language and Culture Committee at the Southern Ute Reservation have helped many people to understand Ute culture and traditions. Without the patient help and support of historian James Jefferson, the first edition of this book would have been filled with inaccuracies. Arthur Cuthair and the Norman Lopez family at the Ute Mountain Ute Reservation have been most accommodating.

We all owe a debt of gratitude to the Bureau of Land Management in Colorado and Utah for their research, publications, and concern for our cultural resources. My sincere gratitude to the Thorne Studio and the staffs at numerous historical societies, libraries, museums, and art galleries in the United States and England that have answered my many letters and otherwise assisted me in the search for virgin information and Ute artifacts.

Jack and Mary Ann Davis, R.T. Wetzel, and John Calantonio have gone beyond all bounds of friendship in allowing me to travel with them for many weeks while doing research in Colorado, Utah, Arizona and New Mexico. Jim and Claudia Eley have graciously provided me with books and manuscripts that would otherwise have been unavailable. Moe and Molly Fleckenstein have kept my husband and many of our Ute friends happy and well fed with delicious take-home dinners.

Patricia Penman and Elaine O'Dowd have been wonderful companions and assistants as we traveled through Ute country and to Washington D.C. interviewing Ute people and searching museums and libraries for the revision of this book.

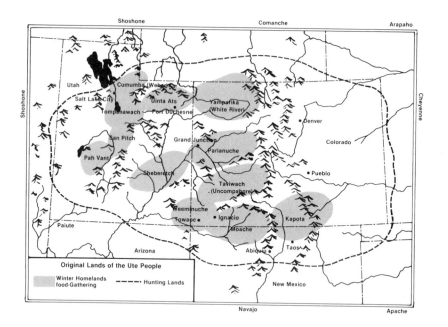

Original Lands of the Ute People

The Ute people have lived in this area longer than any other tribe. Their ancestors could date back 10,000 years or more. Currently the Ute Nation is comprised of six major bands: Uintah, Uncompahgre, White River, Kapota, Moache, and Weeminuche. Some band names have been lost with time and as the bands joined together in larger groups. The state of Utah is named for the Utes.

Preface

The Ute people are reluctant to have outsiders delve into their records. They have been deceived many times and for many years. The first edition of this book contained materials collected from the earliest and best documented records that were available. There was little input from Ute people except a correction of information they felt was inaccurate. Material from the first edition has been combined in this edition with stories and quotes from many Ute sources. Added to this are insights from my personal experiences and current individual concerns for the future of the Ute people and the universe.

The Ute people always seem be giving to those who seriously search for understanding. They patiently answer all questions. Sometimes what they are saying at the time seems to make perfect sense, and yet I often leave wondering what has really been said. During all the time that I have been striving for a quick and easy understanding of Ute culture, my faithful friends have patiently taught me, without my realizing what they were doing, that there is no easy understanding of Ute life. At the same time they have gently led me back to share their belief that the quality of daily life depends on a constant and strong belief in our Creator and Christ as the core of our lives.

My intention is not to create controversy about the Ute people in the past, the present, or the future. What has or has not happened to the Ute people or their ancestors cannot be rectified by feelings or statements of denial or guilt. We must all look to our Creator for the path to peace and contentment with ourselves, our neighbors, and the world we live in.

"Red Ute" Eddie Box, Sr., Southern Ute Bear Dance and Sun Dance leader and spiritual advisor. Photo c. 1960.

Introduction

As a Ute man from the Moache and Capota band, I would like to say welcome to my land. My people roamed all over this country. They had a trail that they traveled from the Eastern Colorado plains area over several mountain passes. These passes were traveled by members of the Sioux band and the Cheyenne and Arapaho, and those people from the plains area knew that they were in the Ute country. According to some of the stories that were told when I was a young boy, my people traveled over those passes quite a bit. They gathered together to go buffalo hunting and went back to the lower country when winter was approaching. Today some of the roads follow the same Ute trails established by the elders a long, long time ago.

When we get up to the top of a pass, we all go out and offer tobacco so that we can travel back and forth with no problems. The Indian people don't just take what we are given without saying thanks. We offered remnants of buckskin, tobacco, calico, necklaces, and whatever we have at the springs and passes. We carry something to offer when we travel over the mountains. We always have and still do.

The reason for offering that blessing was to make sure that we will never be without water. We are aware whenever we are traveling that when we look upon these things like the mountain stream that we as people can make it disappear, if we have no regard for the growth on our land and the resources we have. We have to be aware of what has been provided for those we call the two legged. We cannot take everything. We have to leave some for the next generation. If all the people would be aware of that, we would have continuous resources provided for us.

In order to do that type of thinking, we have to make offerings in place of what we take, so that we will be provided for over and over again. We want you to recognize when you go through this beautiful country that we have here, that when we first see it we know it's beautiful. But if we stay here long enough, we start thinking in different ways: What can we get out of it? That's where some of the problem starts.

We can keep it so our grandchildren and their children will enjoy what we are enjoying now. Take what we can use, leave the rest as it is so our grandchildren can enjoy it. Ah-we-ah-rah. So long my people.

"Red Ute" Eddie Box, Sr.
Southern Ute Indian Reservation

Chapter 1
In the Beginning

In historic times, the Ute Indians occupied the mountains and valleys of Colorado, Utah, and parts of New Mexico and Arizona. Not as tall as the Sioux, Cheyenne, or Arapaho, they were a hardy, vigorous race characterized by high cheekbones and a deep copper-colored skin. They called themselves "Nuche" meaning "the people" or "we the people." The Spaniards called them "Yutas," and the Cheyenne called them "Black People." They were known as the "Rabbit Skin Robes" by the Omaha and Ponca, and "Deer Hunting Men" by the Zuni. The neighboring Pueblos referred to them as the "Mountain People." They were respected and feared by the surrounding tribes.

The Ute language belongs to the Shoshonean branch of North American native languages, which includes languages spoken by Paiute, Chemehuevi, Hopi, Comanche, Bannock, and Shoshone peoples. The Ute language is part of the Uto-Aztecan language family, which includes Nahuatl, the language of the Aztecs. An old Toltec legend from Central Mexico mentions the seven Caves of Aztlan in the "old red land" known as Hue Tlapallan. Near Manitou Springs, Colorado, the red soil abounds in caves. Could this be the area referred to by the Indians of Mexico?

John Wesley Powell spent several months studying the Ute language in the 1870s. He noted, "An interesting fact is that there is no word signifying rich or poor as having to do with much or little property. When an Indian says 'I am rich,' he means 'I have many friends.' 'I am poor' means 'I have but few.'"

Early association with Spanish and Mexican explorers and traders is evidenced by Spanish words and combination words that have eased their way into the Ute language. A source of pride and a symbol of cultural preservation, the Ute language has survived the efforts of outsiders to destroy it. The language is still commonly spoken and understood by most Utes. In schools where the language was once forbidden, there are now Ute language classes for the younger generations, and other efforts are being made to encourage the use of the Ute language. The Southern Utes have published a Ute dictionary and the Uncompahgre Ute have compiled a book of words and phrases.

John Wesley Powell and Tau-ruv stand on a buffalo robe for the presentation of a mirror case. Tau-ruv's belt is decorated with Spanish pesos, most likely obtained in trade with trappers or traders. Powell visited the Uintah Valley Utes in the early 1870s. He recorded Ute lifestyle, customs, and living condition in his diary while his photographer, John K. Hillers, captured some of the most valuable portraits of Ute lifestyle ever taken. John K. Hillers photo, Powell Expedition, Smithsonian Institution.

Before Horses

Prior to the acquisition of the horse in the early 1600s, the Utes survived on a meager subsistence. Their lifestyle was the result of a highly successful adaption to their environment. During the year their nomadic wanderings were limited to the area they could cover on foot. Migrations were determined by a knowledge of where and when the resources offered by nature were ready for harvesting.

No food source was overlooked. Snakes, lizards, caterpillars, insect eggs, and even vast swarms of crickets were eaten in season or dried and preserved for winter use. A favorite method of preparing fresh crickets and grasshoppers was to place them in pits lined with hot stones where they were covered and roasted.

As they traveled from place to place the Utes carried food, tools, and other necessities with them. Men, women, and children carried packs wrapped with rawhide ropes by means of a tump-line over the forehead or slung over the shoulders. There are reports of the

"The Utah, Yutas, or Utes, as the name is variously written, are a large tribe belonging to the great Shoshone family who occupy the mountainous portion of Colorado, with parts of Utah, New Mexico, and Nevada. Those living in the mountains where game abounds have a fine physical development, are brave and hardy and comparatively well to do." — From the 1877 Geological Survey report to the Department of the Interior by W.H. Jackson, photographer. Boulder, Semicentennial celebration, 1909. Chief Buckskin Charlie, center. Horace S. Poley photo, University of Colorado.

Utes using dogs as pack animals and to pull travois as early as 1581. The leather pack saddles for the dogs were loaded by the women. The women would hold the dog's head between their knees while loading or adjusting the weight. The dogs were then tied together in strings like pack trains.

Allies and Enemies

As the settlers from the East moved westward, other Indian groups entered the lands occupied by the Utes. All the incoming groups had some effect on the lives of the Utes.

Navajo and Apache (Athabascan speakers). Both groups are believed to have migrated south from Canada on the western side of the Rocky Mountains. Prior to historic times, the Navajos and Apaches entered the Colorado plains from the north. The Navajo moved into what is now northwestern New Mexico. Both tribes were nomadic, depending on hunting and raiding for their livelihood. By 1500 A.D. the Apaches controlled the Colorado plains, hunting buffalo and planting crops in the river valleys of eastern Colorado.

Comanche. In the early 1700s, the Comanches broke away from their Shoshone relatives who occupied the border country between Colorado and Wyoming. Forming an alliance with the Utes, they drove the Apaches south out of Colorado. The Comanche adopted the nomadic plains life, relying heavily on the use of the horse to haul their tepee homes as they moved with the buffalo through Colorado, Oklahoma, and New Mexico.

Arapaho and Cheyenne (Algonquian). Descendents of a farming people living in earth lodges in the Minnesota area, the Arapaho moved onto the Montana and Wyoming plains late in the 1600s. By the late 1700s they had moved to the Black Hills area of South Dakota, where they formed an alliance with the Cheyenne and began moving into the Colorado plains, pushing the Comanche and Kiowa before them. By 1810, the Comanche and Kiowa had in turn pushed the Apache south into New Mexico. With the discovery of gold in Colorado in 1858, thousands of Euro-Americans ventured onto the plains. They occupied former Indian camping sites and indiscriminantly slaughtered the basic subsistence resource of the Plains Indians, the buffalo. Hostilities increased between the Plains Indians and the immigrants. As the Arapaho and Cheyenne moved off the plains into the mountains in their search of subsistence, hostilities with the Utes increased.

All the tribes living on the plains developed aggressive raiding and fighting abilities in order to maintain a territory of their own.

This warlike attitude would cause problems not only for the Utes but for white travelers moving across the plains and settlers claiming land in Colorado Territory.

Origin Legends

Scholars do not agree on where the Utes came from or when they began living in this area. Archaeological evidence neither confirms nor disproves the Ute's claim of occupation for thousands of years. The Utes will tell you they have been here from the beginning.

Migration legends common with most Indian tribes are absent. The Utes do have several versions of origin legends. Almost all Ute tales have animals as principal characters. They believe animals used to talk and act like humans. Coyote appears frequently in the stories. At times he assumes the role of trickster, dupe, or trouble-maker. In this story of Ute origins, he appears as a representative of evil.

Once there were no people in any part of the world. Sinawaf,* the Creator, began to cut sticks and place them in a large bag. This went on for some time until, finally, Coyote's curiosity could stand the suspense no longer. One day while Sinawaf was away Coyote opened the bag. Many people came out, all of them speaking different languages, and scattering in every direction. When Sinawaf returned there were but a few people left. He was very angry with Coyote, for he had planned to distribute the people equally in the land. The result of the unequal distribution caused by Coyote would be war between the different peoples, each trying to gain land from his neighbor. Of all the people remaining in the bag, Sinawaf said, "This small tribe shall be Ute but they will be very brave and able to defeat the rest."

Archaeology

The study of evidence left by humans is the only means we have to gain an understanding of the lives of prehistoric people. Archaeologists have developed successful methods of reconstructing prehistoric lifestyles by studying food particles, tools, and other evidence of human activity. Fortunately archaeological sites in the Southwest are uncommonly well preserved by the long-term dry climates and the relatively late arrival of historic man. Unfortunately,

---

*Many Ute words have several versions of spelling. The Creator's name may also be found spelled Sineuwa, Senawahv, or Sunawavi.

however, we are all being robbed of our heritage by those who "dig" with hands, shovels, or bulldozers to obtain these relics from the past for their own pleasure or profit. Sites and artifacts on public lands are protected by federal law. If you discover such remains, please leave them undisturbed. Report your discoveries to Forest Service personnel.

Many states have developed a unique program for Avocational Archaeology. These programs give novices the opportunity to provide an immense public contribution to the field of archaeology. Contact your state archaeology office for information.

Archaeologists, anthropologists, and other scholars have established that the historic area occupied by the Utes has been the home of prehistoric peoples for more than 11,000 years. On one edge of historic Ute country, the oldest radiocarbon date for cultural materials in North America was found at Danger Cave near Wendover, Utah.

Paleo-Indians were the first human culture known to live on the western plains. The earliest undisputed evidence of these people in the Colorado area is the presence of projectile points found associated with a kill or a campsite that can be radiometrically dated. A large flaked point dated at ±12,000 B.C. (14,000 years ago) received the name Clovis after it was found in a mammoth kill in Blackwater Draw near Clovis, New Mexico. From a site discovered by a cowboy near Folsom, New Mexico, comes the Folsom point dated 9,000 to 10,000 B.C. The Dent site in Weld County, Colorado, was the first site where Clovis projectile points were found in their original positions in association with the remains of the extinct mammoth. This was the oldest and most positive proof of Native American inhabitants in association with the mammoth. At the world-famous Lindenmeier Site on the Colorado plains north of Fort Collins, Clovis points were found and Folsom points were recovered from a Folsom kill. This site provided a more complete picture of Paleo-Indian life with evidence of both short-term and long-term occupation dating to 10,000 years B.C. (see map on page 131).

The lifestyle and the flora where these prehistoric people lived changed only slightly over thousands of years. Small family bands of no more than fifty people of all ages harvested what nature offered. Their homes were rock shelters, skin houses, or in the open when weather permitted. The average life span was thirty years.

Using darts and spears tipped with flaked projectile points, Paleo-Indians hunted the mammoth and tiny camels. Herds of giant bison were stampeded over cliffs or into canyons where they were killed en masse. As these animals gradually disappeared, hunters turned to the modern mountain sheep, bison, deer, elk, and antelope that remain in the area today.

Colorado and Utah have seen many cultural changes. Each change in the characteristics of a culture has been assigned a name by the archaeological community. Several distinct cultural traditions were prominent in this area prior to the historic period.

Archaic Tradition (5000 B.C. to A.D. 1). Hunters and gatherers, living under rock overhangs, eating mule deer, bison, antelope, and several species of rodents and birds. They used the atlatl, milling stones, basketry, rabbit nets, stone drills, scrapers, and bone awls.

Desert Culture (5000 B.C. to A.D. 1). Hunters and gatherers, living under rock overhangs or in caves, using crude brush huts and windbreaks. They ate some large game but small game, such as jackrabbits, provided a regular diet as well as skins for clothing, footwear, and skin food pouches.

Fremont (A.D. 1 to 1300). Best known for their abundant and often spectacular rock art in Utah and the northwest part of Colorado, they used a crude gray pottery, had a well-developed basketry tradition, and lived in small family houses. Crops of corn, beans, squash, and maize were grown and then stored in masonry units resembling granaries.

Common to all the people who occupied the Colorado-Utah area in about 10,000 years of existence was the fact that they occasionally lived on the edge of starvation, relying upon hunting and gathering activities that could be done on foot.

When the Hauser site near Olathe, Colorado, was excavated by the Chipeta Chapter of Avocational Archaeologists, a projected ledge was found that had provided a rock shelter for a group of Indians who camped there and carried on many of their everyday activities. Remains of fireplaces, manos, bone awls, a hammerstone, quantities of stone flakes, points, knives and scrapers, and animal bones were uncovered.

As large game became scarce, the prehistoric cultures settled into individual drainage systems and became fully familiar with the available food in their home area. Gathering enough food for immediate needs and storing enough for winter was essential. Food spoilage due to bacteria, rodents, and frequent movement no doubt created a world of feast or famine that is hard to imagine. Even when food was abundant, traveling on foot combined with carrying ability determined the amount and types of foods that could be collected and transported to the wintering areas. Lack of rain or heavy snows would have a direct effect on food gathering and hunting. Winters could be deadly if stored food didn't last until spring. When the hunters came home empty handed, and the last seeds and dried flakes of meat were gone, the last life-saving meal might be a broth made by parching and boiling skin storage containers.

Thus passed the short lives of generations of people, people as much a part of the landscape as the wind, the rabbit, and the deer, and just as hard to see. Where did these prehistoric peoples go? Were they driven south by drought or invaders to join the Pueblo Indians? Are they relatives of the Anasazi of the Mesa Verde Cliff Dwellings? Did they move east to the plains or are they the ancestors of the Utes?

Stories on Stone

The oldest form of art in the world is rock art. There are three major areas in the world where rock art appears: Australia, Africa, and the American West. Great art of the past has often been inspired by religious beliefs. Perhaps American rock art, in the form of petroglyphs (pecked) and pictographs (painted), had the same inspiration.

Designs on the rocks provide a journal of social, religious, and cultural traits. Wearing apparel, ornamentation, tools, and hunting practices not preserved in archaeological sites are visible, sometimes in living color, on the rocks. They offer a written story of past lifestyles—all we have to do is learn to read them.

Three Kings petroglyph is probably the most elaborately carved Fremont panel in existence. Famous for detail and workmanship in the designs that depict shields, neckwear, crowns, and horns. Some of the paint originally applied over the carvings remains. L.C. Thorne collection, Thorne Studio.

Newspaper Rock in Utah displays a combination of prehistoric symbols and historic Ute rock art, such as buffalo and mounted horsemen hunting deer or elk. In places, the new figures overlay the older rock art symbols. Horses began appearing in rock art around 1830. Photograph courtesy of Jeannie and Dave Donahoo.

There seems to be a definite locational connection between rock art symbols and cultural evidence unearthed by archaeologists. Symbols depicting game animals, mountain sheep, and bear tracks appear more often along migration trails and near springs where hunters may have been successful. Figures with shields, bows and arrows, and other weapons associated with warfare could represent a concern about problems with surrounding tribes or they might be associated with religious or hunting activities.

The portrayal of masculine activities and exaggeration of male genitalia suggest the art work was done by men. Historians indicate the artists might have been shamans. Some art may have had a shamanistic function, and horned and masked figures depicted are believed to represent the shamans. It is felt that comparatively few artists were skilled in painting or engraving on rock by pecking, drilling, or scratching grooves.

Rock art found throughout Utah and Colorado is the strongest evidence supporting prehistoric occupation by the Ute people. According to archaeologist William Buckles of Southern Colorado State College, "Some rock art styles clearly identifiable as historic Ute manufacture differ little from earlier prehistoric styles of art." The continuity of the rock art styles is noticeably affected by changes in Ute lifestyle. For instance, scenes depicting the hunting of deer and sheep by a lone hunter on foot appear often in the oldest rock art styles. None of these earlier rock art styles depict bison hunting on foot and yet they are similar to Ute panels that depict hunting bison on horses. No other Indians except the Utes were known to live in this area after horses were introduced. George Beckwith was told in 1931 by Utes in Sevier County, Utah, that rock writing was *wee-noose-a-pope,* meaning writing by ancient Indians or old-time Indians.

Sai-ar's family pose before their elk skin tepee in the Uintah Valley, Utah. Judging from the display of beautifully decorated beadwork martingale and saddlebags on the horse, Sai-ar's bandoleer, and other decorated clothing, Sai-ar was a successful hunter and warrior. John K. Hillers photo, Powell Expedition, Smithsonian Institution.

◆
◆ *Chapter 2*
◆
◆ Tepee Culture

The first historic records of the Utes before and immediately after they obtained horses are the written observations of explorers, trappers, and traders who ventured into Ute country.

These early visitors brought gifts to appease or to trade with the Indians they met. These goods included metal knives, axes, arrowheads, and cooking utensils, woven blankets, colored beads, mirrors, and ribbons. These items were quickly integrated into Ute culture. This first acceptance of trade goods would open an avenue for thousands and thousands of whites to enter into Ute country, initiating changes that would have profound effects on Ute lifestyle and the land they considered their territory.

The Spanish began colonization of New Mexico territory in the late 1500s. They brought with them the animal that was to completely change the lifestyle of the Ute Indians—the horse. The Spaniards had no intention of providing the Indians with mounts, quite the contrary. They had laws forbidding all Indians to ride horses. Also prohibited by law was trade with the Utes. Several traders were fined for breaking this law. As late as 1778, a "Bando" proclamation prohibited settlers and "friendly" Indians from visiting the Utes for purposes of trade and barter. Still, a few missionary groups, military expeditions, and illegal traders ventured into Ute country.

Franciscan explorers Father Antanasio Dominguez and Father Silvestre de Escalante traveled through Ute territory in search of a route from Santa Fe to Monterrey, California, in 1776. The Utes were well aware of the value of trade by the time the Franciscan fathers arrived. Near Naturita, Colorado, Father Escalante's men met a group of Utes who offered tanned deerskins and other articles for barter. Escalante traded some of his staples and also gave the "Yuta" two hunting knives and sixteen strings of white glass beads, which they in turn gave to their wives. In return, Escalante received dried venison and two plates of dried berries of black manzanita, described as "very savory and similar to those of a little grape."

Finding Utes to trade with was often a challenge. Some reports described the Utes as extremely curious, coming out to meet the newcomers. Other reports referred to the Indians as unusually shy. Hiding from human intruders would not be difficult for the Utes. They were masters at blending into the landscape while stalking game. Their earth-tone clothing and dark hair provided ideal camouflage. If flight was impossible they could always crawl into a clump of sage brush or fold up on the ground with the hope of being mistaken for a rock. They could drop into a gully and be far away before anyone could catch up with them. The Utes were well known for being able to retreat quickly and disappear into the vast wilderness of their homelands.

Warren Angus Ferris was trapping in Utah in the 1830s when three Utes made a visit to his camp.

> They were stark naked, and betrayed an almost total want of intellect, which was, perhaps, the result of extreme wretchedness and misery, to which they are continually exposed, from infancy until death. . . . Severe hunger instinctively taught them to make us understand that they wanted something to eat. We gave them carcasses of two beavers, together with the head and feet of a dog, which they warmed a few moments over the fire and devoured with wolfish avidity. . . . The barrenness of their country, scarcity of game, compel them to live by separate families either in the mountain or in the plains.

The next day Ferris wrote of another encounter with these same Indians that were supposedly lacking in intellect.

> Four of these Indians came into camp bringing to my surprise, several deer skins to trade, they tried to trade for one of the horses, finally offering them for provisions but were equally unsuccessful.

He also observed their pursuit of food:

> Women and children are employed in gathering grasshoppers, crickets, ants, and various other insects, which are carefully preserved for food, together with roots, and grass seed. From the mountains, they bring the nuts which are found in the cones of the pine, acorns from dwarf oaks, different kinds of berries, and the

W.F.M. Arney was special agent for Utes and Navajos in New Mexico. After complaints from the principal chiefs of the Navajo Nation, Arney was removed from his last agent post in 1874, when he was Navajo Indian agent at Fort Defiance, Arizona Territory. Museum of New Mexico.

Former traders and trappers like William F.M. Arney (second from left) were often appointed as agents or interpreters. The aid they could give their charges was limited. Arney received orders from the commissioner of Indian Affairs in 1849 suggesting, "In dispensing presents to the Indians you will be as economical as possible and confine the disposition of them to cases where some important end is to be accomplished." Salary for the agent that year was $1,500. Museum of New Mexico.

inner bark of the pine, which has a sweet acid taste, not unlike lemon syrup. In the meantime the men are actively employed in hunting small animals, such as prairie dogs, squirrels, field mice, and larger animals or birds. They take fish with simple instruments of their own invention.

The first permanent trade fort in Ute country was probably one called Reed's Trading Post located near Delta, Colorado, in the early 1820s. St. Louis fur trader Antoine Robideaux had taken over the post and was living there with several Indian wives when the bottom fell out of the fur market in the 1840s. The Utes reportedly had an argument with Robideaux and burned this fort to the ground and another belonging to him at the junction of the Uncompahgre and Gunnison Rivers, sometime between 1841 and the exploration of the area by John Gunnison in 1853. Other traders were run out of Ute country around this time because of the decline in fur trade. The Utes had learned that trade goods could be obtained for furs. Now their furs were virtually worthless and they felt the traders were cheating them.

Acquisition of Horses

The acquisition of quantities of horses changed Ute lifestyle faster than any other event in their history. The style of Ute homes changed as did the quantity and quality of clothing, food, weapons, and the nature of Ute social structure. Mounted Utes were able to hunt and kill great numbers of bison on the plains. They could transport their belongings, food, and heavy hide homes over long distances. The mounted Ute quickly developed what is referred to as the "Tepee Culture." A Spanish document of 1720 referred to the Utes as being "like itinerant nations who today dwell in one place and tomorrow in another, and carry with them tents of bison hide to camp."

In the 1820s, trapper William H. Ashley tried to buy seven horses from the Utes.

> These people were well dressed in skins, had some guns, but armed generally with bows and arrows. Their horses were better than Indian horses generally are east of the mountains and more numerous in proportion to the number of persons . . . Such is the value they set on them that I with difficulty purchased two.

The Comanches, who had acquired horses by trading with the Eastern Utes, were becoming a serious threat to the Utes without

The Utes were the first western Indians to have horses in great numbers. The horse completely changed their lifestyle. They were able to travel, raid, and hunt long distances from their camps. They became renowned horsemen, and were considered wealthy and feared by neighboring tribes. Smithsonian Institution.

horses. The unmounted Utes began banding together into larger communities for protection. They traveled from place to place on foot with the women at the front and sides of the group, carrying shields of elk and buffalo hide that Indian weapons could not penetrate. The men followed with weapons ready for use. Inside the ranks were the old men and women, children, and dogs loaded with supplies. In case of attack, the women would quickly form a circle of shields around the men, allowing the men to fire on the enemy without danger of being injured. When the Utes went forth into battle, it was to either conquer or die. They never allowed themselves to be forced to turn their backs upon an enemy. The Utes prided themselves on their bravery in battle, although war honors were not a part of their culture. Enemy tribes agreed that the Ute was harder to kill than any other Indian.

Ute Life

The Ute name for a home is *kan-ne-ga*, meaning a sitting or staying place. Camp was generally made on a hill or high spot within walking distance of a spring or stream. Homes were established in a grove of trees that would furnish protection from storms and offer an abundance of firewood.

When John Wesley Powell visited the Utes between 1869 and 1873, they lived in a variety of homes. The Northern Utes were living in government-furnished canvas tents. Those in southern Utah and Arizona were living in wickiups.

Wickiups

Escalante reported that the most common type of permanent shelter was a domed willow hut, about fifteen feet in diameter and eight feet high, covered with willows, juniper bark, and grass or tule. The low entrance was closed with a flap of twined bark or tule. In the center of the house was a small fire pit for warmth. Most of the cooking was done outside when weather permitted.

Piles of brush would serve as a windbreak for temporary camps as well as a supplement for regular winter camps. Domed brush shelters were likely covered with earth and skins for permanent shelters during winter. Leather-covered tepees did not become practical until after the introduction of the horse.

The temporary camp shelters called wickiups were in use before and shortly after the acquisition of horses. They were erected by using a pole foundation similar to a tepee. Several wickiup sites were studied by Lowie in 1924 and other archaeological surveys in Utah and Colorado.

Brush shelters built in tripod or domed styles were used as temporary dwellings when traveling, for summer use, or as menstrual huts. Brush, tule, or cedar bark was laid or woven through the pole foundation. Cedar bark used on more permanent domed winter huts was matted down to make a good weatherproof roof. L.C. Thorne collection, Thorne Studio.

The structures have a framework based upon a forked stick pole placed on the west end of the structure. Other poles were placed in the fork forming a framework, or tripod upon which other poles rested. On the exterior of the structure there are small branches lying in a circle around the structure which appear to have been green branches used as part or all of the covering. On the interior there was a small fire pit and fragments of cedar bark which could have been part of a bed.

Wickiup villages were found on mesas, benches, or other promontories but never directly at springs or along streams. An average of five persons is estimated to have lived in each wickiup. One village would have a possible population of about fifty-five persons. Artifacts found in wickiups confirm historic reports that a woman would sit at the side of the tent by the east-facing door while her husband sat at the rear of the structure facing the door.

Although brush shelters and shade houses continued to be used into historic times, the pattern of small wickiup groups living together in isolated areas disappeared with the acquisition of horses, which gave larger groups the ability to travel with their tepees.

Using the materials on hand was considered the best way to do things. All three tepees in this photo are attached in some manner to the growing trees with poles supplementing the frame in the same manner that wickiups were built. No matter how dwellings were constructed, the door and smoke holes always face the east. Western History Department, Denver Public Library.

Tepees

The tepee was the woman's home. She made it, she put it up, she took it down, and she moved it from camp to camp. Men living in the tepee were her honored guests and were treated accordingly. Women sat by the door of the tepee on the north side. The man sat in the rear facing the door so he could see who entered and have clear access to the door if an emergency arose. Visitors took corresponding positions according to sex and whatever honorable place the owner of the tepee might give them.

Family rules of etiquette provided the eldest man with the seat of honor, opposite the door of the tepee. He was always served first and always first to start a conversation. Any person who took a drink, ate, or lit a smoke before offering these to an elder (man or woman) would become old before his time.

Horses that were considered the property of the women were used for riding, packing, and dragging the travois that carried the heavy hide tepees when camp was moved. Hides of elk or buffalo were sewn together with long strips of sinew to form the cover. Ten or twelve elk hides were required to make a medium-sized cover. By the late 1890s the shortage of hides for tepee construction required the government to supply the Indians with materials for canvas tepees.

Tepee entrances almost always faced east, to welcome each new day. East was usually the best direction for protection from winds. Ute tepees required twelve poles, including the two used on the flaps to regulate the smoke hole. Tall, thin lodgepole pine, aspen, or cedar trees were preferred for poles. "We always use a three pole tripod to set up now. They could have used four a long time ago," said one Ute elder. Poles had to be replaced several times a year due to damage sustained when moving camp. After the cover was in place, the sides of the tepee were staked down.

When camp was to be moved, boys drove the horses into camp and the women dismantled the tepees. They tied poles on each side of the horse, laid the folded cover over the extension of the poles behind the horse, stacked their belongings on top of that and moved slowly to the next campsite.

Horace S. Poley, a Colorado Springs photographer, sent three sets of photographs he had taken of Ute women erecting tepees to the Smithsonian Institution in 1913. Poley explained that one set "was of Mrs. Buckskin Charlie—he being the war chief of the Utes." One set of plates shows the erection of the tepee of John Robinson, who made his appearance upon the scene just when everything had been completed. The other series is of this same band, but was

"First, four of the best and
longest poles were selected,
and then bound together by a
rawhide rope. This was
wound around them several
times about two feet from the
end and firmly tied. Two
women would then take these
poles and raise them to a ver-
tical position, the tied ends
uppermost. The loose ends
would then be separated in
the form of a tripod and the
poles would be perfectly rigid.
A little at a time, one woman
would open them out to full
diameter excepting two of the
poles would be left about two
feet apart to form the entrance, facing the east."

"Directly opposite these
would be raised a pole to
which the top of the canvas
had been firmly fashioned.
The rest of the poles were
then placed in position, being
supported by the crotches
formed by the tied poles."
Horace S. Poley photos,
Smithsonian Institution.

"The canvas was then deftly brought over the poles, being stretched from both sides toward the entrance; and fastened to the poles at the sides of the entrance so as to leave enough to overlap the opening when the tepee was closed."

"Just above the entrance are two triangular shaped flaps or wings used for ventilation and to let the smoke out. The size and direction of this opening being regulated by two long poles reaching the ground at the back of the tepee. Having adjusted the entrance to her satisfaction, she [Emma, wife of Buckskin Charlie] entered the tepee and moved the poles outward until the canvas was stretched tightly over them. The lower edge was next securely fastened to the ground with wooden pegs. She then fastened the overlapping canvas, between the entrance and the ventilating opening with about half a dozen wooden pins the size of a lead pencil. The lower one of these she fastened a kite-shaped canvas screen that completely covered the entrance. She stored away all the luggage of her family around the edge of the tepee, leaving all the central and higher portion for their unobstructed use." Horace S. Poley photos, Smithsonian Institution.

taken one year earlier in their camp in Monument Valley Park, Colorado Springs.

Smithsonian ethnologists were impressed with Poley's "close observations and true ethnologic instinct." According to ethnologist James Mooney, "That the tepee is built around four main poles is of importance. The Cheyenne, Arapaho, Kiowa, and Sioux build around three poles. The Comanche and some northern tribes build around four as do the Utes, as here described."

Descriptions of setting up a tepee are from an essay that accompanied Poley's photos, entitled *A Ute Indian Camp.*

A band of about seventy Utes under the leadership of Chief Buckskin Charlie had left the reservation at Ignacio, coming by train to Colorado Springs. They brought their finest toggery and tepees with them, as they were to be the feature of the annual "Shan Kive" (good time) of the Pikes Peak Region.

They were taken to the Garden of the Gods where their camp was to be located, (at) a sort of natural amphitheatre, surrounded by red sandstone rocks of huge size and fantastic shapes. Chief Buckskin Charlie selected a site for his tepee on the east near the natural entrance to the camp. (Buckskin Charlie's tepee was the only one painted with a design on the outside.) The other tepees were arranged by twos or threes around the camp according to the fancy of their occupants. The men scattered in every direction, climbing about the big rocks and seemingly enjoying the beautiful scenery as the squaws proceeded to make camp. Old women and young girls dragged the heavy poles and rolls of canvas to the site selected for their tepee, and then went about erecting them.

When the women were ready to move camp, the young boys would bring the horses needed to load the tepees and supplies. A witness to a camp move in 1873 described the procedure.

The Utes were moving camp with 400 ponies, many superb animals. Tent poles, six on either side, were fastened to the ponies of the squaws, one end of each pole dragging on the ground behind. The squaws attend to loading and packing the animals. On the top of many of these packs were perched papooses, strapped securely on, but old enough to drive and guide their ponies.

Chase Mellen, brother-in-law of Colorado Springs founder General Palmer, recalled the Indians leaving their annual summer camp near his home at Glen Eyrie (outside of Colorado Springs) in the late 1800s. He wrote, "I can vouch for the accuracy of that picture of Indian ponies loaded with the squaws and camp equipment, flanked by lodge poles trailing on the ground with baskets strapped securely between, holding the papooses. I can vouch for the truth of the story that when moving camp for a serious purpose the old and decrepit were left behind to die."

Trapper Warren Ferris lived among the Utes in 1834. Describing his own camp he said,

> Our camp was eight leathern lodges and two constructed of poles covered with cane grass . . . Our hunters made daily excursions in the mountains and always returned with the flesh of several black-tail deer . . . frequently killed seven or eight individually, in the course of a day, consequently our encampment or at least the trees within it were soon decorated with several thousand pounds of venison. One who has never lived in a lodge would scarcely think it possible for seven or eight persons to pass a long winter agreeably in a circular room, ten feet in diameter, having a considerable portion of it occupied by the fire in the center. Indeed they are as comfortable as they could wish to be. I moved from a lodge into a comfortable log house, but again returned to the lodge, which I found much more pleasant . . . These portable dwellings are partially transparent, and when closed at the wings above, which answer the double purpose of windows and chimneys, still admit sufficient light to read.

General Palmer's well-bred daughter Elsie recalled her visit to a Ute friend's tepee with a little different opinion.

> Once we and some of the grownups were invited to a feast. My eyes still smart at the recollection of the smoke-filled tepee. The meal was cooked over an open fire in the center and the smoke was supposed to find outlet in the aperture at the top. I well remember the look of the meat, dipped out of a pot and handed to each of us with great ceremony. We were bound to eat or be guilty of unendurable insult to our hosts. It looked the color of an elephant's hide and was just about as tough.

The dragging of the poles on the ground made a very broad track that was used year after year until the path became a well-worn road. Following the routes of the forefathers became a sacred experience for the Utes. They always followed their forefathers' path no matter how worn it became. These "Lodge Pole Trails" became wilderness highways followed by explorers, prospectors, and freight wagons. Many of these old Ute trails are the routes of present-day highways.

Ute Pass Trail

One of the oldest documented routes of any of the Native Americans is the Ute Pass Trail that followed the front range of the Rocky Mountains from the plains into the mountains. Near Colorado Springs the route winds through the Garden of the Gods, where the Utes often spent their winters, and on to their sacred springs at the present town of Manitou Springs. Adventurer Frederick J. Ruxton described his visit to these springs in 1847.

The basin of the spring was filled with beads and wampum, and pieces of red cloth and knives, whilst the surrounding trees were hung with strips of deer-skin, cloth, and moccasins. The Indian regard with awe the "medicine" waters of these fountains as being the abode of a spirit who breathes through the transparent water, and thus, by his exhalations, causes the perturbation of its surface.

Colonel Long's expedition stopped in 1820 at the foot of the trail for a buffalo rib picnic before climbing Pikes Peak. They noted that the "large and much frequented road passes the springs and enters the mountains, running north of the high peak." If Long had been in the same spot nearly one hundred years later he would have seen a group of Ute people ride down the same trail in 1912, as they dedicated it to all those who had passed before. Horace S. Poley photo, University of Colorado.

Chipeta had ridden 150 miles on a pony and 300 miles on the railroad from her Utah Reservation home to Manitou Springs, Colorado, to visit her friend Mrs. Charles Adams and to mark the route of the Ute Pass Trail. They met as young women when Charles Adams was agent and his wife taught school at the Los Pinos Agency. Now they were both widows, so much in common, so different and yet good friends. 1911 photo, Colorado Springs Pioneers Museum.

War Chief Naneece carries a lance as a symbol of peace as he travels down the Ute Pass Trail in 1912. At the top of the hill before riding into Manitou Springs they stopped and broke off chokecherry branches symbolizing peace before riding into the neutral territory of the sacred springs. The Utes stopped at the springs where they gave offerings and asked for blessings before continuing on to a ceremony at the center of town. Anne Cusack Johnson photo, Ute Pass Historical Society.

In 1912, the El Paso County Pioneers organized an effort to mark what was left of the ancient Ute Pass Trail with fifteen white marble markers that were to be placed in a ceremony attended by the Southern Ute Indians. Getting the marble markers engraved with the letters U.P.T. and placing them along the old trail marked in 1911 by Buckskin Charlie and Chipeta was the easy part. Having the Utes attend the 1912 celebration was not so easy.

The town of Colorado Springs was host to an eight-day carnival in 1911. The carnival committee had asked for a group of Ute Indians for exhibition at that event. The good citizens were informed by the Commissioner of Indian Affairs that he did not favor the promiscuous employment of Indians in Wild West Shows. He was, however, not opposed to their employment in exhibitions of a historical and elevating character. The carnival officials were further in-

Ute men performing a Moon Dance surrounded by spectators at the 1911 Colorado Springs Carnival. Their superintendent was reluctant to allow them to attend the 1912 celebration, as dancing was not allowed by the commissioner of Indian Affairs. Horace S. Poley photo, University of Colorado.

formed that they would be required to enter into a contract with the Indians engaged providing for payment of the salaries and expenses of the Indians. After posting a bond and agreeing to pay expenses and to pay each adult Ute five dollars, the Utes were allowed to attend the celebration accompanied by a reservation employee.

The Indians apparently performed dances and other ceremonies that were discouraged at their reservation. These events were so popular with those attending the events that the name of the celebration was changed in 1912 to an Indian name, Shan Kive (good time), with the hope of having more Utes attend.

School Superintendent Werner of the Southern Ute Agency was opposed to the Utes' presence at any further carnivals, fearing they would revert to their old habits. His protest began a round of letters sent between Cato Sells, commissioner of Indian Affairs, E.E. McKean, superintendent at the Southern Ute Agency, and Fred Matthews, general freight and passenger agent for the Florence and Cripple Creek Railroad and chairman of the Shan Kive celebration. After a great deal of political pressure had been applied, a bond was posted agreeing to pay the expenses for the party of fifty adult Indians and their families, paying each adult one dollar in cash and vowing to prevent the Indians from procuring intoxicating liquors in any form, the Utes were allowed to leave the reservation and attend the celebration. Despite Werner's objections, the con-

Moon Face and Eagle Eye at the Garden of the Gods, for the dedication of the Ute Pass Trail, 1912. The Garden of the Gods, near Colorado Springs, was a favorite wintering ground for the Ute Indians for many centuries. Triangular beadwork on leggings is typical Ute style. Virginia Stumbough collection, Ute Pass Historical Society.

tract allowed them to be employed in exhibitions of a historical character, live in tepees, wear costumes, and give exhibitions in dancing and singing.

On the morning of August 29, 1912, the Utes were driven in cars up the Ute Pass road that parallels the old Indian trail. Former Governor Alva Adams, Buckskin Charlie, and State Senator Irving Howbert left their car in the center of the little village of Cascade where they had a short ceremony, each one making a speech and placing a stone as the beginning of a cairn at the first trail marker.

"The procession started down the trail from Cascade toward Manitou, a colorful procession," recalled Frances Heizer, the daughter of Cascade's founder. "The braves in their buckskin suits and feathered war bonnets, and the women greatly adorned with turquoise and silver jewelry. The Indians needed no guides. All the Indians were gay and happy. They chatted in the Ute language and were singing their songs. Buckskin Charlie, chief of this tribe, had not been over the trail since the Utes had left this country over thirty years earlier. His birthplace was the Garden of the Gods and he remembered every turn in this trail he had ridden since a boy. 'I'm seventy years old,' he said. 'I never so happy in all my life.'"

Maude McFerran Price, curator of the El Paso Pioneers Museum, recalled the importance of the pass. "H.A.W. Tabor, destined to be the great Silver King of Leadville, and his wife traveled up Ute Pass in 1860 on their way to Leadville. Yesterday through these grand old Rocky Mountains, the moccasined feet of the red men wore a pathway which proved to be a roadway to civilization. Today the trail lies marked forever, not alone by marble tables, but by the hopes and fears and joys and tears of the fast disappearing race of red men."

♦ Chapter 3
♦ Ute Lifestyle

The food of the Utes consisted of a wide variety of vitamin- and mineral-rich edibles provided by Mother Nature. They ate nuts, seeds, fruits, plant stalks, bulbs, roots, and the inner barks of trees. Many mammals, birds, reptiles, fishes, and insects were other important food sources.

Harvesting, preserving, and cooking were usually considered women's and children's work. Boys and girls learned how to do everything together until they were ten to twelve years old. Boys learned what plants were edible and to cook and sew, girls learned to shoot a bow and arrow, snare a rabbit, and build a shelter. Every person needed to know the basics of surviving with the materials available to them if they were lost or left alone.

Harvest

Women and children harvested vegetation as it ripened. They gathered serviceberry, chokecherry, squawberry, currant, gooseberry, raspberry, elderberry, sour buffalo berry, buckthorn berry, and wild rose hips in season. Some were eaten immediately, others were mashed, with or without their seeds, dried in the sun, and stored.

"They had to go and pick berries during the spring and summer when everything was ripe," recalled Frances Ankerpont in a 1989 interview. "They had to pick their own chokecherries and mulberries. They had to pick some kind of roots for their tea. Today they couldn't do it. Some of them don't grow anymore. We all had to get out there and pick them, the family, little kids they had to help. You didn't just play. Grind the berries, with the seeds, dry them, [make] them like hamburger patties. They still do that today."

Isabel Kent, in a 1985 interview, told how her mother taught her to pick berries.

You pick them at a special time, sometimes when it's really ripe, you don't have to work at it. You just pull it and it just falls in your hand. You can do that when it's ripe, but when it's not ripe, you just have to wait. Or sometimes with certain berries, you just put a cloth underneath and you just kind of tap the leaves with a stick and the berries just fall. That's another technique used a long time ago.

My Mom used to say that the tree is given to us by God. He's given us berries. He's given us all kinds of animals, big, small, and the little ones. If you've seen a chokecherry tree, it's all filled with berries and the birds and animals will not touch it unless you and I go and pick and say "Oh, this is good." The birds then have a right to eat it. The upper part is for the birds. The middle part is ours, the human's, the rest, the bottom part is for the animals that cannot climb. That's why we were taught that we don't pick the whole thing. We leave some, because God gave us this wonderful food, not just for the human beings but for all of us. So we have to share with the little birds and little wild animals at the bottom.

Seeds of grasses and flowers were gathered by brushing the seeds into baskets or onto pieces of buckskin with willow branches or small woven fans. A large conical basket that would hold two or three bushels of seeds was carried on the back where the seeds were placed from time to time. It would take two to three hours to fill a basket.

Seeds were parched on flat basketry trays by placing a handful or two of powdered charcoal or ash over them. The ashes and seed were then tossed in the air so that the chaff would be carried away by the wind or blown away by mouth. A day's labor could result in about a fourth of a bushel of clean seeds.

The seeds were usually roasted in a tray in which hot coals and the seeds were tossed back and forth for ten or fifteen minutes. This process pops the shells leaving a clean white grain. A nourishing hot grain cereal could be made by cooking the seeds in boiling water in a basket pot. Horn spoons were used for eating this breakfast stew. At times seeds and dried fruit were added to flavor the dried or fresh meat in a stew or in meat cakes. "They experimented with different recipes just like women do today," according to Ute elder Bertha Grove.

One of the most useful plants in Ute country is the yucca (also know as soapweed or Spanish bayonet). The blossoms and seeds are edible. A rich, sudsy soap can be made from the roots, and the fibers in the long dagger-like leaves were used for twine and rope.

Leaves of many plants were used as greens. They were usually boiled with meat. Roots and tubers of plants such as the yampa, cama, wild carrot, and wild onion were harvested with three- to four-foot-long digging sticks. The sticks were cut green, sharpened on one end by rubbing on a rock and hardened by burning the points. Roots were often baked by placing them in an earthen oven made by digging a hole four to five feet long and three feet deep, lining it with stones, and building a fire on top. When the wood burned down, the hot rocks were covered with a layer of damp grass, the roots were placed on the grass, and another layer of grass was on top of the roots. Hot flat rocks were laid on the top layer of grass, covered with a mound of cold rocks and dirt and left to cook overnight.

Mormon settlers, following the example set by the Indians, avoided starvation many times by collecting the seeds, greens, and bulbs of the sego lily. In gratitude, the people of Utah named the sego lily the state flower of Utah. *(Caution: Do not eat plants or roots unless you have positively identified them as edible. Many species are poisonous.)*

Sweet sap was collected in the spring from the pine trees by slashing the tree and inserting a sharpened hollow deer bone into the slash between the bark and the center. The sap was allowed to flow into a bark container and was eaten immediately. When food was scarce, bark was stripped from the trees and the substance inside the bark scraped off and eaten raw or mixed into a mush with other ground foods.

The piñon tree was important to the Ute way of life and diet. The nuts were gathered by knocking them to the ground with a long pole or shaking the tree over a skin placed on the ground. Nuts were eaten raw, or parched in hot coals to remove the shells. What was not eaten was ground into a meal that might be stored for later use, when it could be mixed with water and baked in a cake form in ashes or on hot rocks. These nut cakes could be stored for a long time. Grinding tools are almost always found at collection sites near piñon groves.

Pitch was used as an adhesive to repair sandals, as a sealer for basketry water containers, and chewed as gum, as was the root of rabbitbrush.

Cups, ladles, bowls, and platters were made from knots of wood. Most of these implements had a hole where a thong could be attached for carrying on the belt or saddle. Elk-horn wedges were used for felling trees (for tepee poles or other uses) by driving the wedge into the tree with a heavy stone—a long, hard process. Understandably, metal axes were a sought-after trade item.

Preservation and Storage

Over the centuries, the Utes developed food preservation methods that rival any we use today. Fish, game, nuts, seeds, and berries were preserved by various methods of drying and smoking.

At times pine nuts were stored as green cones since they remained tightly closed in that state and are difficult for rodents to get into. When they were ready to open the cone, they put them in coals to open the cones and secure nuts.

Large grinding stones called *metates* combined with a small handheld stone known as a *mano* were used to crush or pulverize the grains, berries, and dried meat that was stored in skin bags. The women would usually gather together near a tree or other shady spot where they could visit while they worked. When they finished grinding, the stones were turned upside down and left where they had been used, indicating a regular return to favorite campsites.

Although the grinding process was a great way to process food there was one drawback to grinding food on stone: fine grains of sand wore off the stone and were mixed with the food. Consequently teeth were gradually sanded and worn down, which often caused decay and other problems for older Indians.

Skunk Eyes demonstrates grinding done on a thin bedrock stone called a mah-rutch *by the Utes. The smaller stone held with both hands was pushed away from the body with a rocking motion over seeds, nuts, tubers, berries, lumps of salt, corn or meat that was pulverized and pushed off the end of the stone onto a piece of buckskin.* L.C. Thorne collection, Thorne Studio.

This family from Uintah Valley, Utah, photographed in the early 1870s, depended upon the animals and plants around them for their livelihood. Their clothing is made from hides of various animals and decorated with elk teeth and porcupine quills. Their tepee is made from elk hides, and a buffalo robe thrown over the horse made a comfortable saddle or a warm bed at night. Clothing and sleeping robes are airing on a tripod. Corn is drying on a tripod in the background. In the foreground is a painted hide parfleche bag used for storing food, clothing, or other supplies. John K. Hillers photo, Powell Expedition, Smithsonian Institution.

Buffalo, deer, and elk meat was cut into thin strips, sometimes placed briefly in boiling water, and hung on racks to dry. Small fires under the racks kept insects away, added flavor, and hastened the drying process, which might take two or three days. Bones of deer and possibly other animals were pounded and boiled for grease, which was then stored in balls mixed with dried and pulverized meats. Meat was stored in skin sacks with or without the fat. "In the old days a skin bag would hold about a hundred pounds of dried meat," said one Ute elder. Strips of dried meat were stored in a folded rawhide bag called a parfleche. Berries were never added to the stored meat. They were dried, mashed, and formed into balls for separate storage.

The Indian suitcase, or parfleche, could be used for storing food or clothing. Parfleches were made from hides that were not tanned, called rawhide. Rawhide was made by stretching deer or female buffalo hides on the ground. The hide was held taut with stakes while it was scraped and left to dry. Designs were painted on most clothing bags but food bags were usually left undecorated.

Many types of skin sacks were used by the mounted Utes. Mounted Utes tended to use two skins joined together and held open with a willow hoop rather than a basket for gathering seeds and berries. Scrotum sacks were popular. Every woman carried a skin sack on her belt to hold her awl.

Cooking

Venison (deer meat) roasted on a stick next to the fire was the preferred fresh meat. The Utes might eat only once a day, but their usual meal times were in the morning and again in late afternoon. Hot rocks placed in a rawhide bag about one foot in diameter, made a fine cooking pot. A pot or kettle of meat was put on the fire, and flat breads were cooked on a hot rock. When ready, the meal was placed in the center of the floor, where everyone could help themselves by dipping into the pot with knives, fingers, horn spoons, or a clay or wood bowl.

FRY BREAD RECIPE

2 cups flour
½ tsp. salt
2 tsp. baking powder
⅛ tsp. lard
Enough warm water to make a ball of dough

Mix flour, salt, and baking powder with warm water to make a dough. Knead the dough until it is soft and does not stick to fingers. Allow to stand thirty minutes. Pull off a chunk of dough about the size of a medium apple. Form into ball. Pat down on floured board. Shape into flat pieces by stretching with hands until about 1/16-inch thick. Poke hole in middle so the spirit can get out. Fry the pieces on both sides in hot grease. Serve plain, or with honey, chili, or eggs.

Cooking fry bread and corn on the cob at the Uintah-Ouray Reservation c. 1920. Fry bread is a staple for almost every meal. Ute women sit in ceremonies with their legs tucked under and to the side in this fashion. L.C. Thorne collection, Thorne Studio.

Basketry

Other than the fish traps usually made by men, basketry was done by women using either a twined or coil weaving method. Sleeping mats were made of willows laid in rows and twined together. Burden baskets, parching trays, seed beaters, jars, and hats were made in the twined style. The favorite method for basket making was the coiled style used for water bottles, trays, and bowls. No colors or decoration are found on this early basketry except, on occasion, a coat of clay.

Three-leaf sumac, sometimes referred to as "squawbush" or "skunkbush," was preferred for coil baskets. New sprouts of green sumac twigs were cut in the fall. A twig was held in the teeth as the bark was peeled away. The remainder of the twig was split into three slender strips and the pith immediately removed with a sharp knife or stick. A heavier stalk (coil) would be used for the framework. The peeled strips (weft) wind around the coil, forming the body and pattern of the basket. "I used to help my Grandmother make this kind of basket," a Ute elder told me. "We used skunkbush or willow, soaked it, and had to hold it in your teeth and pull the strips off with both hands. Long strips of bark. And split the willow to make the inside of the basket. Had to have good teeth to do all this."

Ute elder Isabel Kent reported that the Utes gathered a certain kind of willow in the fall when the twigs were very flimsy. For bas-

Wedding baskets were made by the Utes for trade with the Navajo. They are always the same general shape, design, and color. According to one Ute woman, "Everything has a meaning. The circle at the center of the basket might represent the earth. The red line between the black stars is life. The (black) star is something like 'Thunder Beings' or something to guard." An open road called a "Spirit Line" is always made in the design. This opening allows the spirit of the basket to go in and out. When making the basket, the last strip of weft on the edge should stop at the open road. *Museum of Western Colorado collection.

Small and large water baskets were made by the women from willows collected in the fall. The basket is made watertight with sap from pine trees. Handles on the large basket are wooden. Small basket handles are braided horsehair. Don Stotts photo, Archer and Jordan collections, Ute Pass Historical Society.

Filling water baskets was a daily chore done by the younger women early in the mornings. Water left in the baskets overnight was considered "dead water," not suitable for use. Stale water would be poured gently back onto the earth and replaced with fresh water. L.C. Thorne collection, Thorne Studio.

Two Ute women, Pooques on the left and Red Rope on the right, weave baskets in front of a brush shelter. Dried willow twigs from the bundle between them are bent into a coil, holes are made with an awl, and thin, softened willow strips are woven through the holes to hold the coils together. Baskets were made watertight with a coating of warm pine pitch applied on the insides. Berries are drying on the hide behind Pooques. L.C. Thorne collection, Thorne Studio.

kets used in Sun Dance ceremonies, no metal tools were used, only natural materials. Water baskets were made during the winter when the women were sitting around and talking. These baskets were sturdy and waterproof. For waterproofing the baskets, a certain kind of sap was boiled until it was very sticky. Small round pebbles from the river bed were added when the sap was poured into the basket, and the basket was rolled around and shaken so the pebbles would work the sap into the grooves of the basket.

Pottery

The Utes made very little pottery. Small amounts of crude pottery shards and few whole pieces have been found at prehistoric and historic Ute campsites. Some of the vessels found within the areas occupied by the Utes probably indicate trade between the Utes and the Navajos during the nineteenth century. Ute pottery is usually in the form of water cups and cooking utensils. Moving pottery from one campsite to another without breaking it would undoubtedly require special efforts for nomadic people.

The majority of Ute pottery was made from a mixture of lime, clay, sand, and manure ground into a powder. The powder was moistened and kneaded into a dough-like substance, rolled into a rope about one inch in diameter and several yards long, and coiled from the bottom up into the intended shape. Cooking pots were tall and broad in shape, and had two holes in the top where a leather handle could be attached for carrying while traveling. No slips, polishing, or decorative painting was done on early pottery.

Hunting and Fishing

Ute men spent the majority of their time hunting, fishing and making the tools necessary for the pursuit and capture of game.

Fishing provided an easy source of protein for all Utes. For those living near Utah Lake, fish was a primary source of food. Unfeathered arrows or spears, handmade lines, and hooks of bone or wood were used for fishing in shallow water. Dipnets or basket traps were used when the fish moved upstream to spawn. Fish not eaten immediately were split down the middle, so the backbone could be removed, and laid across two poles to dry. Dried fish was stored in skin sacks placed in pits lined with bark or grass. The pits were covered with juniper bark and then topped with rocks and dirt to keep the stores dry and safe from predators. Most surplus food was stored in this manner. Dried fish was the only food Escalante was

Notorious Chief Colorow, front row on the right, and his band of Ute warriors visit Colorado Springs on a hunting trip. They have adopted various combinations of traditional Ute and adopted non-Ute clothing items and weapons. This photo was taken in front of B.H. Gurnsey Landscape and Photo Shop sometime before 1882. The Burns Theatre Building was built on this site at that time, but now, like the Ute Indians, it too has disappeared from the landscape. B.H. Gurnsey photo, Colorado Springs Pioneers Museum.

able to obtain from the Indians near Utah Lake. He was able to purchase dried buffalo meat from thirty mounted Utes near Jenson, Utah.

Rabbits were a major source of food and clothing for Utes without horses. Men hunted rabbits with a bow and arrow, sling, throwing club, or with snares made from sinew. Hunters could smoke rabbits out of their holes, or attract them by imitating the cry of an injured rabbit by blowing through an old rabbit skull. Families would often join together for communal rabbit and antelope drives to provide surplus meat, hide, and rabbit fur used in making woven fur blankets and sleeping robes for the long, cold winters.

A leader was chosen for each drive by virtue of his experience and ability to select a time and place where the drive might be most successful. Utah Utes used rabbit nets, using cordage woven from flax secured in autumn from stems of dogbane, Indian hemp, or stinging nettle. The crude nets, with a one-inch mesh, standing three and one-half feet high and hundreds of yards in length, were arranged in a circle supported by stakes and pinned firmly to the

Bandoleers similar to this one were used by men for holding cartridges and for decoration. They were often heavily beaded and painted. This bandoleer was collected c. 1870 by General U.S. Hollister. Denver Art Museum collection.

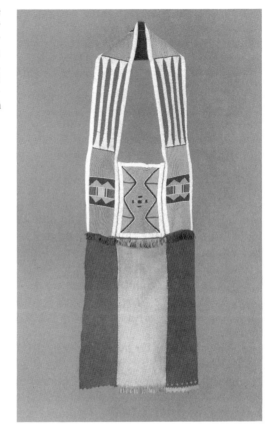

Hunting platforms were common near game trails. This tree platform close to the tepee was most likely used for sleeping or as a lookout to watch for the feared "buffalo soldiers" (black soldiers). Similar platforms were used for temporary storage of food and supplies out of reach of dogs and rodents. Permanent storage caches covered with cedar bark were often built in larger trees. Utes did not use burial platforms. John K. Hillers photo, Powell Expedition, Smithsonian Institution.

ground. Wings were extended at angles from a small opening, continuing for several hundred yards on each side. Brush corrals were occasionally used in the absence of nets. The entire gathering of Indians would begin to beat the brush in the direction of the corral, driving the rabbits through the small opening which was subsequently closed behind them. The game was then harvested by using sticks, bows and arrows, or simply picking the rabbits up by their hind legs and smashing their heads on a log or rock. The Utes of Colorado more commonly used fire to drive rabbits or other game by setting fire to sections of brush, paying close attention to wind direction.

In the fall, when the antelope were the fattest, scouts were sent to locate the herds and a leader was chosen for the mens' communal hunt. A stout corral was built below a low cliff with long angular wings of brush leading toward the edge. The herd was driven into the wings and over the cliff into the corral. The waiting hunters, armed with arrows, spears, or clubs, could kill as many as two hundred of the stunned antelope in a single drive.

The wolf, fox, coyote, wolverine, mountain lion, and wildcat were often considered spiritual brother animals and the source of power for men. They were considered clever and dangerous and were rarely hunted unless food was scarce. When they were killed, only the hides were used and the meat was rarely eaten if other food was available. Badger hides were for used as paint bags. Beaver tail was considered especially good to eat. Beaver were shot as they left their dens at dusk, or the dens were destroyed to capture them.

Buffalo, antelope, and deer hunting was most often accomplished by individual stalking, or by ambush near a watering hole or from a brush covered pit. In the 1830s Ferris reported, "In places where deer are numerous, they excavate holes in the earth, in which they conceal themselves, and shoot them as they pass in the night." The decoy cry of a fawn, made with an aspen leaf in the mouth, might lure a doe close enough for a kill.

According to Guy Pinnecoose, a Ute man interviewed during the Duke Oral History Project, the old way to hunt was to work from the bottom up a hill in the first half of the day and from the top down the second half of the day. "Your wind is coming from the top down in the morning and then when you're coming down, the wind is coming going back up. Lot of hunters don't know this and that's the reason why they have so much trouble when hunting. They don't know how to hunt." Deer were hunted in cold weather by hiding close to their trails or ambushed from a tree blind. In the winter elk were surrounded and driven toward deep snow until they tired and floundered, allowing the hunters on homemade snowshoes to get close enough for the kill. Elk and deer were easily pulled home across the snow on sleds made of the hides.

Mountain sheep were surrounded or driven up a mountain where the hunters waited in ambush. Some hunters were fast enough to run down a buffalo and shoot him in the ribs with a bow and arrow. Elsie Palmer Myers, daughter of Colorado Springs founder General William J. Palmer, wrote of witnessing a similar feat. "We saw a small flock of antelope running along the top of the rocks and a number of Utes clambering up with incredible speed in pursuit. One of the braves caught an antelope by the hind leg."

Major Powell reported that "The flesh of the Grizzly Bear is esteemed very highly. The hunter who succeeds in killing one is considered a great hero. They tell many stories of the prowess of their forefathers in attacking and killing these huge animals. It seems that all the men of the tribe turned out on such occasions."

When a group went out to hunt, the person who killed an animal was entitled to the skin, but the meat was divided equally among all the people. The kill would be brought into camp where the hunter would divide up the game by cutting portions from the animal and giving them to whomever came to get them.

Weapons and Tools

When the men had time to spare, they kept busy by making weapons, tools, and projectile points. Horn bows made from elk, deer, or mountain sheep horn predate the more modern wood and sinew bow inventions. They were made by softening the horn in boiling water or over steam until pliable, splitting it, and gluing end to end to form a single curve. The joint and both ends were wrapped with buckskin and strung with the two- or three-ply sinew bowstring used on all bows. The early Spanish records report that the Yutas had two bows, one of which was seven feet long, tipped with horn at one end and a sharp pointed buffalo rib at the other. This bow could also be used as a spear at close quarters.

The hunting bow used by most men was a double-curved style, four feet long, and one-and-a-half inches thick at the center, made from juniper, chokecherry, mountain mahogany, or cedar. They were made by soaking the wood until it was flexible and then staking it on the ground and leaving it to dry in the desired shape. The back of the bow was covered with a long wide strip of sinew for strength. Both the center and the ends were wrapped with strips of sinew from the legs of deer. The sinew was attached with glue made from mountain sheep horn. Boys just learning to shoot were given a single curved bow usually made of willow.

Arrow making was often a specialty of older skilled men who would trade their work for hides or food. Serviceberry, squawbrush, wild rose, or other berry wood was used most frequently for the two-foot-long arrows. Arrows could be made by rolling the wood between two rocks or by working it with the hands and teeth. The best arrows were made by running the green arrow wood through a large hole in a bone wrench to remove the bark. When dry, the shaft was made pliable by warming near a fire and the arrow was again drawn through a smaller hole in the wrench, with pressure applied as needed for straightening.

Wing feathers from a variety of birds (such as eagle, magpie, hawk, or owl) were attached to a split shaft, fastened with pitch, and wrapped with sinew by the hunter, who would also decorate his arrows with paint, designs, or notches. Arrowheads were attached with sinew, or the end of the arrow itself was sharpened. An old legend explained that "prehistoric points are the scales of armor of a giant . . . when he was killed in the early days, points flew all over the world." Old points were often picked up by the Indians and saved for later use.

Many types of rock were used for making arrowheads. Points made from almost every type of rock have been found. The most common are chalcedony, carnelian, sard, crysoprase, agate, petrified wood, bloodstone, onyx, flint, chert, and jasper and quartz. Arrowheads were made by breaking a large stone into what is called a core. From this core a smaller piece called a blank is struck. The blanks are carefully shaped by holding a tool of bone, antler, hard wood, or softer stone against the core and hitting it with a hammerstone until the point is the desired shape.

Buckskin Charlie (center) holding an unusual weapon. His subchiefs carry their lances and shields of the warrior. 1901 photo, Smithsonian Institution.

Knives were made of flint and obsidian in various shapes and for various purposes. Those used for skinning were sharpened on one edge. In order to apply pressure, the other edge might be padded with a piece of stiff hide.

Quivers to carry the bow and arrows were made by the men from fox, wildcat, coyote, antelope, and buckskin. Arrows were carried in one section and a fire drill might be stored in another section. Men were usually responsible for starting fires with their drill when camp was moved.

Undecorated spears were used for hunting buffalo, while feathered spears were used for battle and ceremony. Forked spears decorated with feathers and strips of cloth were usually carried as a peace symbol. Clubs and axes made of heavy stone were used by some Utes. Rocks, hand thrown or in slings, were often used by boys as weapons to kill rabbits and sage hens or for tests of skill.

Shields made from three thicknesses of buffalo hide were shaped in a mold of sand with hot rocks used for pressure to hold them in place. When formed they were stretched over a frame, painted with symbols, and decorated with feathers and small animal skins according to the beliefs of the owner. They were carried on the back when traveling, while in camp they were hung where they were within reach of the men, usually in front of the tepee along with the spears and other weapons.

War honors for the Utes differ from those of other Native Americans. Raids and war were undertaken not for glory but for loot, and if the loot could be obtained without bloodshed, that was the preferred way. Societies that honored warriors and brave deeds determined who had the right to wear certain types of feathers and colors, or who was given a warrior's name. In this 1894 photograph an attack on a former scout married to a Ute woman was staged for the photographer using an "instrument of torture" found on the site of Chief Ouray's cabin. Horace S. Poley photo, c. 1894, Colorado Springs Pioneers Museum.

Horsemen

The horse became a man's most important single possession, not only for hunting and raiding, but as a status symbol. Horses were acquired by and usually belonged to the men. The men and boys took care of all the horses, even those horses that were given to the women. Horses could be traded for many things, including a wife. The Utes were expert mountain horseman. They were seen loping down steep slopes in pursuit of deer or elk at full speed, over places where a cautious man would dismount and lead his horse. Men and women rode on saddles made of leather bags filled with grass. More elaborate saddles were made of stout sections of pine branches and deer or elk antlers bound together with rawhide strips to form a frame and covered with rawhide. Women's saddles, often referred to as "squaw saddles," were higher than those of the men.

Saddle blankets made of matted horsehair were used under the saddle. Navajo or trade blankets were laid over the saddle for riding. The horse was directed by the rider's knees, and/or a single rein of braided horse or buffalo hair used as a hackamore. Leather bridles were prized possessions, usually obtained by trading buckskin to the Navajos. A foot stirrup, made by braiding a loop of horsehair into the mane, was used to enable a man to hang on the side of his horse and shoot under the neck when fighting. Horses were sometimes painted for special occasions or decorated by braiding feathers and beads into the mane and tail.

Mountain parks, waist high in grass, provided ample grazing for growing herds of Ute horses. One trapper noted that horses were permitted to run loose, making them easy prey for marauding Arapahos. Cheyennes and Arapahos began raiding into the mountain parks, allegedly to hunt bison and other game but more frequently to plunder the Ute horse herds. The Utes defended their mountain homeland fiercely, taking possessions and scalps from the invaders at every opportunity. Few skirmishes were lost to the trespassers. In 1847, the English adventurer George Frederick Ruxton and his guide Killdeer followed a group of "Rapahoes" traveling on foot, their only equipment being lariats to steal horses. Ruxton pushed on ahead and warned his Ute friends. After the Utes had dispatched their enemies he joined them in a victory celebration.

If pasture was scarce during winter, the Indians would feed their horses on the bark of the sweet cottonwood, a food upon which the horses not only subsisted, but fattened. The salted inner bark of the pine tree might be used as food for the Indians under similar conditions.

Following a fight, scalps were displayed on poles like banners while the women chastised the scalps telling them they should have stayed home and not come to Ute country to steal and cause trouble. If a woman had lost a son or husband in the fight she might be given a scalp. Some scalps were attached to a warrior's bridle, but most were left on poles outside the tepees—a flag of prowess. Smithsonian Institution.

Buffalo Hunters

Buffalo (bison) hunting on a grand scale and eagle feather war bonnets appeared in Ute culture at the same time. Both were symbols of power and success for the mounted Utes. Hunting bison was becoming more and more important to the economy of many tribes. Bison provided so much in one package they are often called the "Indian Supermarket." The meat tastes good and is low in fat and cholesterol, and although the Utes didn't know the buzzwords for healthy food, they did know what foods were good for them.

The introduction of the horse to western Indian tribes made a definite impact on the Great Plains and interrupted the Utes' isolated lifestyle. The Utes had hunted small herds of bison in the mountain parks of Colorado and the Great Basin of Utah, but nowhere was the bison hunting as significant as on the plains. The Utes were not alone on the plains—other groups from far and near converged on the plains where bison was the most sought-after source of staples for mounted Indians. The Utes, Comanche, and Shoshone occasionally formed alliances when hunting or raiding on the plains as protection from other groups.

Having a good buffalo horse was important to the success of a hunt. A good fast buffalo horse could run alongside the buffalo while the rider speared or shot the buffalo in the ribs. Butchering was done on the spot by cutting from the top of the head, down the middle of the back. The tongue was usually saved for the feast after the Bear Dance. The hide, brains, liver, and other choice parts belonged to the killer, while the remainder was divided among the other hunters. The kidneys and livers of all big game animals were eaten raw. The testicles were cooked before being eaten. The back muscle (sinew) was carefully removed, cleaned, and hung to dry. It was later twisted into a thread which was very strong and long lasting. If there was no danger from enemies the women did the butchering. An elder Ute woman told me, "They didn't have to, they wanted the things done right so they did it themselves."

Buffalo hides were tanned mostly by the women, and were favored for blankets, winter robes, and tepee covers. The strong buffalo hair was often braided into a four-strand lariat. Cups and ladles were made from the horns of buffalo or young male mountain sheep by heating the horn near the fire or in hot water until it could be set into a mold in the ground, shaped with a bone knife and filled with earth to preserve the shape while drying.

Eagle Catchers

Men and boys often captured eagles and kept them tethered as pets. Adult eagles might be caught from inside a brush-covered pit by using pieces of meat on top as bait and seizing the bird by the legs when it landed. Sometimes the eagle was killed by wringing its neck, but usually the tail and wing feathers were plucked and the bird was released. When a nest was located, the eaglets were often frightened out of the nest by flapping a blanket, or a young man might be lowered on a braided rope to retrieve the fledglings from the nest.

A favorite Ute story tells of a young man who was being lowered into an eagle's nest by his father when the rope broke and the young man landed in the nest. Stranded, he ate food brought for the eaglets. When the two eaglets were old enough to fly, he tied himself to them and they lowered him, uninjured, to the ground.

Eagles were captured and raised on a diet of rabbits. This photo was taken in the Wasatch Mountains of Utah around 1874 of Nau-no-kwits and Ku-ri-en and their eaglet lashed by the leg to his tree roost. When the eaglet matured they would harvest the prized feathers used for decoration and ceremonies. John K. Hillers photo, Powell Expedition, Smithsonian Institution.

Eagle feathers, pipes, and paints were given to a person who had earned the right to have them or use them. Buckskin Charlie, Chief of the Southern Utes. Lisle Updyke photo, Delaney collection.

The privilege of wearing eagle feathers was something an individual had to earn. "Men and women alike earned the right to wear these highly prized symbols of the spirits in the sky," according to Ute elder Bertha Grove. "The first feather you got was not of your own choice but given to you. In those days people had to be given the right to have eagle feathers and the right to pass on feathers." These rights were earned by performing brave deeds or given to recognize feats of endurance. "The way I earned my plumes was my grandfather gave that to me, at Bear Dance during the last endurance dance with one partner."

Men wore the feathers, and women usually wore the fluffy plumes. The golden eagle feather was a woman's feather. The red hawk is known as the "little brother eagle." Its feathers are often used in eagle-feather headdresses. Other birds, such as doves and owls, were hunted for their meat or feathers using a bird arrow that had no point or had a short piece of wood attached crosswise near the end of the arrow. Hunters were known to test their skill on the quick little hummingbirds.

Clothing

Clothing styles and materials vary among the Utes. Each person, group and time period had a distinctive general style. The quality and quantity of clothing depended upon the resources available. Women made most of the family's clothing, although men would make some of their own ceremonial and hunting clothing and accessories.

Written in the diary kept by Escalante and Dominguez in 1876 is this passage: "Eight Indians approached us . . . most of them were naked, having only a piece of buckskin on their pudenda." Considering the warmth of most clothing made from animal hides, it doesn't seem unusual that these Indians would be barefoot and scantily dressed in warm weather. The lack of clothing was considered "shockingly unsuitable" by a culture used to keeping their bodies covered at all times.

Father Escalante made careful notes concerning the clothing of the Utes he encountered. He wrote, "Very early twenty Indians arrived at the camp—wrapped in blankets made of skins of rabbits and hares."

Rabbit skins were woven into warm blankets when buffalo robes could not be obtained. The preferred winter robe was of buffalo hide, with hair left on the outside, tanned on inside and painted with designs. Robes were also made from badger, woodchuck, coyote, and gray wolf skins. Where deer and elk were not available, clothing was made from antelope hides, which lacked the lasting quality of buckskin.

Vegetable fibers were used for clothing, shelter, blankets, basketry, and footwear. Sandals were made of yucca fiber, sagebrush bark, or muskrat hides tied together at the toes and heels and lined with softened sagebrush bark. In winter, leggings made from twined sagebrush bark provided protection from the cold.

Women wore loose dresses with open sleeves made from two doe or antelope skins or three mountain sheep hides. More modern styles with an attached or separate yoke required an additional skin.

Prehistoric clothing was plain with little or no decorations except fringe, paint, a few elk teeth, and occasionally porcupine quillwork. Hand-fashioned bone beads were worn as necklaces or attached to clothing. As trade beads and other trinkets became available everyday clothing was often beaded along edges and yokes. Geologist/explorer John Wesley Powell noted, "It is curious the effect civilization had on women's dresses . . . worn so long now they trail upon the

Ute women were very important to the economy of the family. They tanned hides, dried and stored food, and made and decorated most of the clothing. The woman in the center has trimmed her buckskin cape with elk teeth and beadwork. Several are wearing shell ornaments and bone chokers as well as various medals and award ribbons. The woman on the right has painted or tattooed her cheeks with a circle broken by a horizontal line. The woman at the top is Emma Naylor Buck, the wife of Chief Buckskin Charlie. The woman in the center is probably her mother (A-pat-we-ma) and the other girls are her sisters (Towee, Cegre-che-ok, and Tachiar). Henderson photo, Western History Department, Denver Public Library.

ground . . . fringed with furs and beaded with elk teeth . . . beads are replacing the porcupine quills."

Ceremonial clothing was heavily beaded. Shell casings, buttons, and Mexican coins were popular decorations. Some women's dresses might have a hundred or more elk bugler teeth. This was a sure sign that her husband was a good hunter, as each elk has only two of these teeth. Trade cloth and hide clothing combinations were seen as early as 1870. By the turn of the century, hide clothing was worn only for ceremonies and special occasions.

Headwear for women in cold weather might be a scrap of buckskin worn like a bandanna. Men wore round caps of beaver, muskrat, or weasel fur with the tails hanging down at the back. Children had fur hoods for winter wear.

Small children often wore nothing at all on warm summer days until they were about six years old. Very small children might have a belt with a long loop that could go over the mother's shoulders. In case of danger, she could pick the child up, sling him over her back and run. Children's clothing was usually made from smaller animal hides like fawn or rabbit.

Women's everyday working clothing was usually very plain. A cape made from a separate hide covered the shoulders. This cape worn by Shi-ra-sa, wife of To-ka-wah-ner, is decorated with elk teeth and a strip of porcupine quillwork down the arm. The tail of the animal the cape was made from is centered in the front of the cape. John K. Hillers photo, Powell Expedition, Smithsonian Institution.

Pah'-ri-ats, in the Wasatch Mountain of Utah c. 1873. His shirt is a longer style worn by the Utah Utes. He is wearing the fringed buckskin with the V-neck flap seen on all Ute men's shirts, a breech cloth, leggings with long, long fringe, and plain moccasins of a type worn before 1880. Hanging on his belt is a beaded bag. He holds his bow case and decorated quiver. Decorated clothing was worn for special occasions. John K. Hillers photo, Smithsonian Institution.

Women wore moccasins and knee-high leggings, either separate or attached. The moccasins shown are attached to the leggings, which have beadwork only above the ankle. The plain moccasin bottoms were typical for everyday use prior to 1880. After that time moccasins were more heavily decorated and the leggings were usually much shorter and separate from the moccasin. Blackmore Collection, Museum of Mankind, London, England.

This photograph was mistakenly labeled Chipeta (Ouray's wife), by the original photographer, and this woman does bear a strong resemblance to Chipeta. Most historians think she is Susan, Ouray's sister. Her cape is decorated with beautiful quill and bead work. The large belt is decorated with a U.S. Army buckle, coins, and chains. Her hide dress is painted, beaded, and heavily fringed. A wealth of silver Navajo trade bracelets covers her arms. She is displaying the possessions of a woman with a successful husband. Colorado Springs Pioneers Museum.

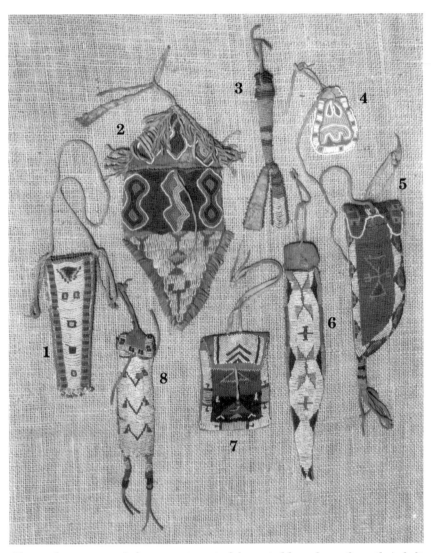

Men and women carried an assortment of decorated bags hung from their belts and over their shoulders. Women always carried a knife bag and usually carried an awl case to hold their awl made from deer cannon bone, sharpened by rubbing on a stone. The awl was used for poking holes in hides when sewing, for making baskets, and many other uses. Tools and other essential items, such as awls, needles, and knives, flint, and steel, were carried in these bags.

   1. Possibles bag   *5. Knife bag*
   2. and 7. Ration card bags   *6. Paint bag*
   3. Awl case   *8. Knife bag*
   4. Personal bag

Don Stotts photo, Ute Pass Historical Society collection.

Subchief Dick Charles and son. Children's clothing was styled the same as that of adults. Boys did not have the V-flap on shirts until they became adults. This young boy has a small whip—boys often had small replicas of adult weapons. Colorado Springs Pioneers Museum.

Adornment

Both men and women would decorate their bodies and their clothing with paints. Natural earth paints mixed with marrow fat were applied to the body for ceremonies, appearance, and protection from the elements.

Northern Ute elder Frances W. Ankerpont remembers, "The elderly people, wherever they went they find a pretty color of the earth, they have to pick it up. This earth was made for us to use when we're living here on this earth. We believe that when you take something from the earth you have to pray for it." Pigments from the earth were ground into a fine powder. The Utes traditionally used pigments from the earth rather than vegetable dyes. Ankerpont notes: "Women had red earth for rouge. They have to pray to get it so they can use it. I have to put some little bit [of dark red

Women's and children's faces were often decorated. The color and designs used all had a special purpose or meaning. Traveler Ida Riddle wrote about one Ute woman she noticed at the Ute Agency at Ignacio in 1903: "The parting of her hair was painted bright yellow and it seemed she had an extra amount of red paint on her face." H.H. Tammen photo, c. 1902, Brigham Young University.

rouge] on my cheeks every day. You do a prayer when the sun comes up, pray for good wishes for family to do good, then all day long it's with me. We use the dark red."

Adventurer George Frederick Ruxton noticed the use of paints to celebrate a victory, "Paints, vermillion and ochers, red and yellow were in great request, whilst the scraping of charred wood, mixed with gunpowder, was used as substitute for black, the medicine color." Black was used around the eyes to prevent snow blindness, while yellow or white clay used on the face or body in a solid layer

John (Yellow Flower), a Yampa Ute warrior, was well known and admired by white settlers and his people. Typical of young Ute men, he wore a bead in the part of his hair and otter fur braid decoration. Trade cloth and buckskin are combined in the typical fringed men's shirt decorated with a V-flap in front. The sides of the flap are usually decorated with a bands of quill or beadwork. It is very unusual to see a decorated V like this one. John died suddenly at the Hot Springs in Middle Park, Colorado, in 1873. Blackmore Collection, Museum of Mankind, London, England.

might have a design scratched into it. At different times of the year men and women painted their faces with red clay mixed with deer fat to protect the skin from the sun and wind.

"An older guy can have yellow," said one Ute elder. "Men prefer red everything. They have to blend in. I guess they had to earn colors. They've lost all that tradition."

Tattoos and ear piercing were sometimes performed on children by a grandmother or older woman using cactus thorns dipped in the ashes of burned cedar leaves. Males were tattooed only on the forehead with an oval design, a cross, or a semicircle, while the females might have a circle on the forehead, a semicircle over each eyebrow, or horizontal lines across each cheek.

Men and women washed their hair and clothes with yucca-root soap and bathed in streams, natural hot springs, or sweat baths. Hairbrushes were made of bundles of grass or yucca, while a porcupine-tail comb could be made by inserting a handle into the tail and charring the quills to an even length. The traditional hairstyle for women was hair parted in the middle and worn loose, with no decoration. Around the turn of the century younger women started braiding their hair in a style similar to that of the men.

Men parted their hair in the middle or on the side and usually separated it into two sections that were braided or wrapped. According to their position in life and the honors they had obtained, they could wrap their braids with otter or weasel skins, or attach feathers or beads to their hair for special occasions. The men usually removed all of their facial hair by rubbing with ashes, plucking, or scraping with a knife.

Tanning

Utes were well known for the fine quality of tanned hides they produced. The inner surface of the hide was scraped clean of fat and flesh with a chisel-shaped flesher made from elk antler, a buffalo tibia, or elk or deer cannon bone (the large bone in the lower leg). The hide was hung by the head on a slant pole frame for scraping. Heavier hides were stretched on the ground. The hide was washed, soaked, rinsed, and wrung out, and then boiled animal brains, stored in intestines or bark containers, were rubbed thoroughly into the hide with the hands, a small bunch of juniper, or hair. After drying in the sun for a few days, the hide was again soaked, rinsed, and wrung out by twisting with a stick, then again hung out to dry. The long, tedious process of stretching by holding the hide with the feet and pulling toward the body took half a day or more. Heavy hides might be further softened by rubbing with a stone or pulling a sinew rope back and forth over the surface.

Hides intended for women's clothing were left white. Men's hides and hides for tepees and various bags were hung over a tripod for a final fifteen- to thirty-minute smoking. Smoking was usually done early in the morning when the air was still, using a fire of greasewood for turning skins yellow, willow for brown, and pine for a light yellow coloring.

The hair was left on buffalo robes used for sleeping or winter robes. The tanned side of robes was usually painted with colors made from natural earth or vegetable dyes applied with a pointed stick wrapped with sinew. Hides were cleaned by rubbing a white clay into the skin with a flat stone and then shaking the clay out when it dried.

Camp at Ignacio. Women made the tepee covers by sewing together ten or more elk skins or fewer buffalo hides with long strips of sinew. H.S. Poley photo, Smithsonian Institution.

Whiterocks trader, William A. Samuelson, operated a trading post on the Uintah-Ouray Reservation from 1889 to 1893. While there he collected beaded buckskin articles including this beautifully beaded traditional ceremonial dress. Every color, and even the type of fringe design, on the dress had a meaning to the person who made it. According to a Ute elder, the designs are a very old style. The blue background might represent the sky, the red (dark areas) represents Mother Earth. The dots on the sleeves could mean people. The center design with bands extending over the sleeves represent a bird with the central dots radiating from the circular waist area representing morning or day. The shoulder designs tell something about dancing. Samuelson collection, Utah Field house of Natural History State Park.

♦ *Chapter 4*
♦ Traditions

The constant quest for survival kept the Ute people in top physical condition. Those who reached maturity were the fittest of their race, masters of their environment and well equipped to provide for their family.

A typical family unit consisted of the father, mother, children, grandparents, and the husbands of the daughters. The eldest man in the family was usually recognized as the headman to acknowledge his greater experience and his ability to provide good advice.

An individual might live with another band but he would still retain membership in the band of his mother. These close family ties fostered common ownership of food and supplies. The hunters' game and the women's harvest was shared with the elders and others not able to provide their own livelihood. Sharing of food and other supplies was taken for granted. If anyone asked for the possession of another person, the polite thing to do would be to give that person the item. For this reason, it was not considered polite to ask for or to admire other people's possessions. Trapper Ferris was amazed at this attitude of sharing. "When I would give none of my possessions to one he turned to one of his companions and observed, 'That man's heart is very small.'"

Material possessions and horses were privately owned. While leaving the village to steal from other Indians was considered necessary, stealing from a guest in camp or another Ute was highly unusual. Theft was the sole unpardonable crime, and the penalty for theft was usually a complete loss of all personal possessions. A man could be dismissed from the band along with his entire family, while a woman was beaten and turned out of the village alone.

Village Life

A band or village was made up of varying numbers of family units. Small groups traveled together during spring, summer, and autumn. Several groups often gathered for three or four months in a permanent winter camp and in spring for celebrations. General Rusling, traveling through the West on an inspection tour of army posts in 1866, described one village as having three hundred tepees arranged almost in streets. "Shelters of hides, shields, and spears [were] left at entrances . . . One could not move around the village without having scores of dogs yelping."

George Frederick Ruxton described another village:

> Numbering some two hundred or more lodges . . . erected in parallel lines, which covered a large space of the level prairie in the shape of a parallelogram, in the center . . . the space . . . was left unoccupied, save by one large one [lodge] of red-painted buffalo skins, tattooed with the mystic totems of the "medicine" peculiar to the nation . . . From the center lodge, two or three medicine men, fantastically attired in the skins of wolves and bears, and bearing long peeled wands of cherry in their hands, occasionally emerged to tend a very small fire . . . Before each lodge a tripod of spears supported the arms and shields of the Yuta Chivalry and on many of them, smoke-dried scalps rattled in the wind.

Marriage

Marriage was a priority in an economy that relied upon the combined efforts of a man and a woman to survive. Men and women had roles of equal importance in family life. Every person was attached to a family unit and had a specific function to perform. Couples who were incompatible simply changed partners to preserve the harmony that was so necessary in a small group. Children almost always remained and still do remain with the mother or her family.

A man might live with more than one woman, since a man who could afford it might have more than one wife. A second wife would often be a sister or other relative of his first wife. He might be responsible for other women living with him as well, such as his wives' relatives. Women might have more than one husband or have other men living in her tepee if circumstances warranted it. These men would usually be related and not considered husbands. Due to economic considerations this was not uncommon.

It was not acceptable to marry anyone who was a blood relative,

"The Warrior and His Bride" is the label placed on this photograph taken by John Hillers on the Powell Expedition in the Uintah Valley. The men would prepare for a wedding or other special event by painting their bodies. This man has covered his entire body with white or yellow clay and then scratched patterns into the clay. John K. Hillers photo, Powell Expedition, Utah State Historical Society.

not even a cousin, but a man was expected to marry and care for his brother's widow unless she was considered "no good."

Adultery was condemned. A jealous wife, sometimes accompanied by friends or family, might take aggressive action against a rival; taking her possessions, killing her horse, cutting her hair, physically assaulting her, or challenging her to a wrestling match with the victor winning the man. The wife might still give her husband away after this action or she might injure his horse as a way of rejecting him. A man could reclaim a wandering wife by physically removing her from the other man's presence, sometimes ending with the woman in the middle of a tug of war. A man generally wouldn't attack another man in such a case, but he might take the rival's possessions or kill his horse, thus giving up the right to reclaim the woman.

Sai'-ar and his family sit on a buffalo robe with their daughter, who has been dressed up by her proud mother with at least seven trade bead necklaces and a bracelet on each arm. Her father appears to be a successful warrior and hunter, judging by his clothing and the bandoleer over his shoulder. John K. Hillers photo, Powell Expedition, Smithsonian Institution.

Even during reservation days men looked for outside help to control their wandering wives. One man wrote to Washington to ask the president of the United States, whom he referred to as his father, to help him get his wife back from a man who had taken her.

A girl was considered ready for marriage after the first of her menses. The first menses was a special occasion in a young girl's life. She would inform her mother when this started and be taken to a small brush menstrual hut away from the camp. Her mother, aunts, grandmothers, or other older women would spend the next ten days advising the girl on proper behavior. At the menstrual hut, she would be encouraged to rise early in the day. She was kept busy with vigorous work, such as running to get water and picking up wood for the fire, thus insuring that she would always be industrious. She was told to drink lots of hot water, avoid salt, and not to eat meat or her skin would darken. She was taught not to touch her face with her hands but to use a scratching stick to prevent wrinkles and keep her hair from falling out. After a massage and a bath in yucca suds or sage, the girl was dressed in new or clean clothes and her old clothing was given away.

The monthly visit to the menstrual hut was a social experience when several women might stay together. They would grind seeds or sew moccasins and visit. Making baskets was forbidden during menses, as it was thought that splitting twigs would cause the teeth to fall out. The man was warned to avoid contact with the women at this time or it would endanger his power and might make him sick or shorten his life. For a married woman to eat meat, or even to cook meat, during her menses was to invite bad hunting for her husband. Despite all these rules governing behavior in the menstrual hut, it was not uncommon for a lover to sleep with a woman in the hut, especially when courting.

A boy was considered a man and ready for marriage when he was able to provide meat. His first big game kill would be given away after he was rubbed with the blood of the animal. Deer blood would make him fleet of foot, the coyote's blood would make him shrewd and hard to deceive, while the mountain lion's blood would help him to be strong and able to follow tracks. This ceremonial bath of blood was followed by a great deal of advice concerning marriage and life. He was told to be good, to never quarrel, and that partners in marriage should do things for each other. He should never let the sun catch him in bed. The old men would say, "If you're going to be lazy, you won't be worthy." A poor hunter or horse raider might have difficulty in obtaining a suitable wife.

A girl could not be forced to marry. Her parents might try to influence her in the choice of a first partner by suggesting a man who was a good hunter. In some cases an agreement might be made between parents for their children to marry when they were of age. In most cases, the children knew this was to be the case and did not oppose their parents' wishes.

The practice of obtaining a wife would differ from area to area. A suitor could offer presents to the family, or he might move in with the family and hunt for them to prove himself capable of providing. A young man might just move in and lie next to the girl he wished to marry. Her mother often sat up all night until dawn when the man would leave, to make sure he did not touch the girl. The mother might throw dirt in the suitor's face and tell him to leave. He would repeat this night after night until the mother tired of watching him. When a man moved in to sleep with a girl, it would constitute marriage; in later times having a blanket thrown over a couple was considered a marriage ceremony. The couple would remain with the girl's family until they had children and would then start a home of their own.

In other cases, the suitor might bring meat to the family, and if the family accepted it and ate it, he was considered married. In some cases, he might send a friend to plead for him or to offer the

Women wed soon after reaching puberty. A young man had to prove he could provide for a wife and family before he could choose a mate. A courting flute like the one held by Tony Buck was used to court his pretty wife Juanita. "They play a love song that the woman will like," says Eddie Box. "The spirit is making that sound through the flute and the spirit of the woman feels that, just like a love song." H.H. Tammen collection, Colorado Historical Society.

girl's family buckskin, horses, tobacco, and blankets on his behalf. Two suitors courting the same girl might settle the dispute with a wrestling match. The final test before marriage for couples was being "smoked" in a tepee with a small fire and the vent flaps closed. Several hours in this smoke-filled room without dissension meant the marriage would last for a long time.

There are many reports of the Utes trying to trade horses for white wives in the late 1800s. Hester McClung wrote in her diary of such an instance while she and her family were on a "camp cure trip" in 1873.

Yah-man while conversing at our tent door with George surprised us with the following, "Me heap pony—much rich—me one squaw—heap poor—you heap rich—much squaw—me swap pony for squaw." Objections offered only made him more desirous to trade, "White squaw good—swap two ponies," more objections then "Me heap rich—many pony—white squaw heap nice—me like white squaw heap—swap two ponies and a mule." After I answered "Me like Ute—but me like white woman heap"—he gave up. During another conversation with Yah-man about Arapaho, he said "Arapaho scalp made good buckskin—me shoot Arapaho—take Arapaho scalp, me take Arapaho squaw on pony," and quick as a flash he dramatized his words by taking me in his arms and carrying me to his pony. To say that I was a little frightened is expressing my feelings in the mildest possible manner . . . the others told me his eyes were twinkling with merriment, a good joke on the white people.

In another instance, settler John Mandeville related a tale of Chief Colorow trying to barter for John's wife. "What do you think, Clara, Chief Colorow wants to buy you and the baby?" "Buy us! With what?" "Ponies, at first he offered two, then four, then six." "And what could you say to him to make him understand?" "That white men did not sell their wives, of course." "And could you ask him to go away satisfied?" "He went, but came back later with a whole string of ponies, and began all over again. Told me I could have the whole bunch. He wanted White Squaw." "But do you think. . . ?" "He's gone. I think he'll not come back, I told him *no* so emphatically that he disgustedly turned away and rode off with his ponies, flinging over his shoulder as he went, "White man heap damn fool."

Children

There are abundant terms of endearment in the Ute vocabulary for children from infancy to adulthood. Everyone helped to care for the children, and young children were expected to help their elders in return. Grandmothers and grandfathers often spent the majority of their time sharing their knowledge with the young people. Rarely would children be punished by hitting or spanking; instead they received their knowledge and training from examples set by their elders. At times they were told tales of ogres and witches as examples of what could happen if they should wander too far away or otherwise endanger themselves.

Children were expected to behave a certain way. "They won't sleep in," recalled a Ute elder. "I was raised that way. They have to be up when the sun rises. Today I guess they sleep all day. When I was a little girl, we didn't play when we were eating. There was a

Severo's children. Children were indulged, pampered, and seldom spanked. Instead, they were taught by loving guidance and good examples set by their elders. Three boys and a girl are shown in this photo. Boys braided their hair and, as they gained honors, were able to wear beaded strips, beads, or feathers in their hair. Colorado Historical Society.

Capiton and Isareta, two of Severo's children, wear their everyday cloth clothing made in styles similar to buckskin clothing. They always wore moccasins, as did most Utes, even when dressed in white man's clothing. H.S. Poley photo, Smithsonian Institution.

Care of young children was often an accepted duty of older sisters or grandmothers, leaving parents free to do necessary jobs. John K. Hillers photo, Smithsonian Institution.

time to play. When [the adults] were doing something like a talk we had to sit and listen. Today you don't have that. Seems like today they don't want to listen, they don't sit like we did. They want to be moving and playing. All the children are like that, they don't sit. If you try to read to them, they'd rather be doing something else. I would be afraid to do that."

Pregnant women followed customs such as avoiding fattening food to ensure an easy delivery, and avoiding certain meats like

Children spent most of their first year in a cradleboard carried by the mother or an older sister. The boards were usually made by grandmothers from a willow or pine frame covered with buckskin, and were often elaborately beaded, in the style of the girl's toy cradleboard shown here. The beaded strip hanging beside the large cradleboard fastens across the padding to hold the baby's head firmly in place. Ute cradleboards are easily recognized by their twined basketry hoods. Brigham Young University.

beaver that could cause the woman to "dam up" and have a hard delivery. It was thought that too much deer meat might cause the birth of twins, which was considered unlucky. When a woman was about to give birth, several older women accompanied the new mother to a birthing hut, where poles were set in the floor for her to grasp as she knelt during labor. The new baby was washed in yucca suds each day to hasten growth and wrapped in soft sagebrush bark or skins. Baby and mother would sleep in a pit bed kept warm with hot rocks heated and placed under the bed each morning and evening by the father.

As soon as the baby was born, the new father would run up and down hills, a feat he would repeat daily to ensure that he remained quick and lively when he returned to hunting. Until the umbilical cord dropped off the baby, the father would remain at the birthing hut, following the same customs the mother did—using a scratching stick, not eating salt, fat, or meat, and not drinking cold water. When it was time for the father to leave, he would be ceremonially bathed by an elder man, preferably a good hunter, to whom he gave his old clothes as a gift. He might also go on a symbolic or real hunt and give away his first game to someone he wanted the baby to take after.

In early days, the father buried the umbilical cord in an ant hill so the baby would be lively and walk quickly; in later days, the cord was kept in a small bag on the cradleboard until the baby could walk. The cord was then buried. The cord was often left on an anthill when the baby outgrew its cradleboard. If the ants took the cord down into their hill, it was considered a good sign, meaning that the child would go out into the world and mind his own business while gathering food and other things for the tribe. Ute life was thought to be similar to that of the ant, who works and shares his labors for the good of the group.

After the morning bath, the baby was wrapped in a soft mattress of rabbit skin or buckskin filled with eagle down, deer hair, or soft cloth in later periods. To keep the cradleboard clean and contain the baby's wastes, the Utes used packing of cattail down, grasses, and soft cedar bark. Soft mullein leaves were sometimes used to wipe the baby. Sometimes the lacing of the cradleboard was left open or a hole was made in the buckskin cover for the boy's penis to allow urination. Girls had soft bark or a rag placed between their legs with the end hanging out for drainage.

Babies slept and were carried in a cradleboard until they were six months to a year old, but they weren't kept in the board all day. During the day babies were often hung in their cradleboards in the

Women carried their babies in cradleboards on their backs. A board like this one could weigh as much as thirty pounds without the baby. When camp was moved, the board could be fastened on the sides of their horses or on the travois pulled behind the horse. The high back would protect the baby's head if the cradleboard was to fall. Rose and Hopkins photo, Colorado Historical Society.

Medicine bundles with blessing and protection symbols are attached to the side of cradleboards. This bundle on a boy's board has attached to it an elk tooth with a carved tepee symbol, a Palo Alto Pink perfume bottle from San Francisco, California, a round beaded strip with yellow feathers, a green beaded strip, and an umbilical cord. Jan Pettit photo, Ute Pass Historical Society collection.

shady limbs of a tree while the mother worked. Old-style boards had a high back that would protect the baby's head if the cradleboard fell. The most distinctive characteristic of a Ute cradleboard is the willow-work basketry covering that provided shade for the baby's face. There was usually a light covering attached to the hood that could be pulled across the baby's face to keep away insects and to provide a shade while napping.

Cradleboards were often used for more than one baby, if the new baby was the right sex for that type of cradleboard. If the baby who originally used the cradleboard died, the cradleboard was not used again. Boy's cradleboards were white, while those of girls were rubbed with yellow earth paint. Cradleboards are still used by many Ute mothers today. Most modern boards lack the high backs. Babies often fall asleep even while they are being laced into the secure nest of the cradleboard.

"Babies didn't cry so much in the old days when they were in their boards," recalls elder Isabel Kent. "The cradle was their home, they don't feel lost there, you put them in there and they just hush, because they're warm. Their arms are down and their feet are straight. When you carry a baby, their hands and arms are flying all over, and when we put them in there, they have a place in this world that they cannot be doing that. They would hush their babies, like put their finger over their mouth, and kinda tap it, and sing to the baby and cuddle it, and just love it. That's why the babies are quiet when they're with you. They stayed right by you. Our children never cried. But today's children do, it depends on how the parents take care of them. They don't do all that rocking anymore."

Children kept pets, the most common being a puppy. All Utes claim they have never eaten dog meat "like the Arapaho did." Dogs were often related to the wild coyote. Each family had at least one and as many as twelve dogs which were never fed but left to fend for themselves. They provided an excellent warning system as well as keeping the camp area clean of garbage. Other pets might be a hawk or fawn, captured when young and raised by the children.

Young children were given toys that were small replicas of tools they would use as adults. Dolls, animal figures, or other toys were sometimes made of clay burned in the fire. Girls might try making small baskets and cups as their mothers wove larger baskets. The inner bark of young cedar trees was often cut into little strips that were painted with figures of men, women, children, or animals and bound together like a little book. The boys would walk on a type of stilts, shoot their small bows and arrows at a target or through a ring, run races, and climb trees. A favorite game was for children to

Dogs were favorite pets. This young man is obviously proud of his well-bred dog, which may have been obtained through trade or as a gift. Notice the sinew-wrapped bow, arrows, and the trade bead necklace and hair decorations. John K. Hillers photo, Powell Expedition, Smithsonian Institution.

impersonate a deer or other animal to see who could do this best and who could run the fastest on all fours like the animals while the other children tried to catch them. Swings were made of braided yucca fibers and hung from trees for children's play.

Children were taught by older members of the family, not only by their mother or father. Boys learned tracking and hunting and how

Elders were important in tribal life. They were the teachers and the counselors who provided guidance for the young people. Gaining wisdom and patience was an important quest as a person matured. Shown here: Chief Buckskin Charlie and his wife, Emma. Lisle Updyke photo, collection of Robert W. Delaney.

to pick the right kind of wood for a bow. Girls learned camp skills and sewing and helped care for younger children. Gradually they acquired ingenuity, a remarkable perceptive faculty, patience, endurance, and the skills of the elders; they then took their place in society according to their talents.

Death and Burial

Scaffold or tree burials were not used by Utes. They did use platforms for food caches and summer sleeping areas, but platforms were primarily used for hunting, and were usually placed near game trails. Some examples probably functioned as vantage points or lookouts and may have been used to catch birds or eagles or for sleeping in warm weather. Remains of tree platforms are common in piñon or juniper forests. Poles were wedged into the crotches of the limbs and often covered with cedar bark.

Perhaps the Ute custom of burial at cave entrances and in rock crevices is the basis of the Ute story about a dark, gloomy underground passage known as Na-gun-tu-wip where departed spirits dwell. When passing through, owls hoot, wolves howl in the distance, and grizzly bears' footprints can be seen in the sands. At the end of the passage a bridge crosses to "beyond the chasm." It is believed that only the brave can pass through this passage to reach the happy hunting grounds.

The majority of prehistoric burials are pit burials, with the bodies placed in a flexed position. Grave goods were few in number. Male burials are accompanied by projectile points, atlatl weights, scrapers, and other tools associated with hunting activities. Female grave goods usually include manos, metates, hammerstones, choppers, and bone tools associated with gathering and food processing. Infant and young children's burials are often accompanied by more ornamental items, such as stone and shell beads and pendants and/or mammal- and bird-bone beads.

At one western Colorado burial site, dating back to the Archaic period, a woman's body was buried in a pit and covered with a cairn of sandstone blocks and a milling stone. Studies indicates she was 4′8″ to 4′11″ tall and died at about the age of forty. Bone examinations reveal bone scars formed by temporary cessation of bone growth due to infections, starvation, or other factors typical of a hunting and gathering lifestyle. The lines indicate several episodes of bone growth stoppage that occurred during her childhood and adolescent years. A bone awl was all that was found buried with her.

A mid-nineteenth century burial of an adult male Ute Indian was recently located near the site of the Old Los Pinos Agency (near Gunnison, Colorado). He was estimated to have been between thirty and forty years old at the time of death. He had a typical robust stature for Utes, being about 5′2″ to 5′6″ tall, and was apparently a remarkably healthy individual. Burial was in a bowl-shaped crevice in a rock outcrop. The remains were probably covered with pine duff and dirt. Found in the grave site was a white glass shirt button commonly used on shirts as early as the 1830s. Also found was a crown four-inch conch shell with a hole drilled into it, pieces of a native-made saddle, and possibly a deer. His remains were reburied.

In historic times, death was met with various outward displays of grief. Women would cut their hair and wail "loud enough to scare the stock," according to one settler. Men might cut themselves but would not wail. The body was usually wrapped in buckskin and laid in a rock crevice, cave, or gully and covered with brush and rocks. A man's horse and dogs might be killed at the burial site. Favorite personal possessions were usually left at the grave for the owner to use in travels to the next world.

In some bands, the tepee or other living quarters and all possessions of the dead person were destroyed, burned, or abandoned if the person had died in the dwelling. Older customs demanded mourning for four days, believing the ghosts of other relatives were near to receive their new member. A spot of pitch was placed on the crown of the mourner's head to keep ghosts from bothering the living. The mourners would grieve for the deceased until their hair grew long again, but usually would not talk about the deceased. If memory of the departed person was not allowed to die, the living mourner could soon die too.

Providers and Protectors

"The Indian men were the providers, the protectors, the people that were responsible to keep order in the family or in the village or in a camp," says Ute spiritual leader Eddie Box as we sit at the state capitol building in Denver, Colorado, one hundred years after the Utes were moved to reservations. "The real thing was what the warriors did. They provided safe keeping, directed our young people to become good warriors, and provided for and had feeling for our old people—for all the people. That was their responsibility."

When asked if men sat around and smoked all the time, Eddie Box replied with a laugh. "No, that was the only time they probably recognized some of the Ute men, when they were smokin' sitting

Pe-ah (Black Tail Deer), a young chief and distinguished warrior of the Grand River band, wears a combination hide and trade cloth shirt decorated with beadwork. A paint bag and perhaps a peace medal or drinking cup are attached to a hair rope slung across his chest. The long flaps on the bottom of his leggings are made by leaving the hind legs of the deerskin intact. Pe-ah often camped near Denver with at least thirty five lodges and 250 people in his group. Photo c. 1868, Colorado Springs Pioneers Museum.

around." Smoking is not just smoking, according to Eddie. It is a way of offering prayer. "At that time when they smoked they were smoking a peace pipe. They didn't smoke it for the pleasure of smoking. They smoke it for offering. Offering prayers, prayers for the women for what they've done like cooking. This is a man that's offer-

Wa-rets and Chief Shavano. Photo c. 1868, Blackmore collection, Smithsonian Institution.

ing tobacco, offering smoke and they say, for what my women did for me, this is what I'll do . . . I'll be a little more understanding. That was very difficult to do, to understand what good is in everything."

Ute men gathered to talk about hunting or about moving camp, to discuss problems, to sing, and to tell stories. When they gathered to talk, they usually smoked their pipes. Pipes were made from stone, bone, or red rock found near Provo or Duchesne, Utah. In later years, more durable pipestone for the pipe bowl was traded from Minnesota. Pipe stems were made from wild rose, elder, or a hollow reed. The Utes would occasionally set fires and burn an area

Pipes and decorated pipe, tamp, and tobacco bags were carried by every Ute man. They were treasured companions throughout his life and were often buried with him. Buckskin Charlie (center) holds an unusual pipe that would have been given to him as an honor. Beadwork and carvings cover the stem, and rings of silver encircle the bowl. His necklace is a beautiful example of Navajo trade silverwork. His sons hold pipes typical of the style used by Utes. White Wing (left) wears a painted yoke shirt called a scalp shirt because of its hair fringe, which decorates the clothing of both young men. The hair was more often from a horse than human hair. Julian's shirt (right) was made from trade cloth, decorated with a traditional front flap, fringe, beadwork over the shoulders, and scalloped dress cuffs. Gonner photo, Center of Southwest Studies, Fort Lewis College.

to promote the growth of tobacco and grasses. Wild tobacco leaves or the inner bark of the red willow called kinnikinnik were crushed and smoked separately or mixed.

Whenever a pipe is lit, smoke is offered to the four cardinal directions, to mother earth and the grandfather above. "This is a gift to the creator, the creator of the earth, four-legged and two-legged animals and all the grandfather put on mother earth," said one Ute elder. One pipe would be passed in a circle to the left, "in the direction in which the sun travels," each man taking a few puffs; at other times each man might smoke his own pipe. Men rarely smoked during the middle of the day. The most usual time for a man to pull his skin tobacco pouch from deep inside the pipe bag and sit down for a smoke was early in the morning or in the evening.

Chief Pe-ah and other leaders pose with their peace medals obtained by attending conferences with the Great Father in Washington, D.C. The ability to kill large quantities of game with rifles like these Winchesters, combined with increased mobility on horseback, led to closer association between small groups and the formation of larger bands. W.H. Jackson photo, Museum of New Mexico.

Chiefs and Leaders

Ute bands have always joined together for social visits, ceremonies, and weddings. They aided each other when hunting or for protection. Yet, within geographic areas, their customs, clothing, even the food they ate and the methods for obtaining and preparing it, were quite different. The strongest common bond was and still is their shared customs, and religious, social, and ethical beliefs.

Ute social organization varied depending on the size of the group. Several families would be organized into a band. Each band would have one or more leaders. The leader or chiefs of the band were normally older male members who had proven themselves to have good judgement and the ability to lead by persuasion. Where several bands joined together, there would be a principal chief, who was the most powerful and most influential man, as well as a war chief, a hunting leader, and others. At times, the same man could have all these responsibilities.

The band chief usually decided when and where to move the band and to some extent organized the hunting parties. If the bands split up temporarily for pursuit of food, a subchief would be expected to take charge of his group. The chief was not expected to carry all the responsibility for the group. A council of all the leading men would meet often to discuss such questions as places they might move to or where they should collect food or hunt. After hearing all the opinions, the chief would give his ideas and that was considered the decision. If any members did not agree with the decision of the chief, they might leave and form their own band.

The war chief often had little influence on the day-to-day decisions of the band. He was revered for his bravery and prowess, and if he was a man of good judgment he would be expected to lead battles, as well as plan attacks and defense.

The chief usually had the largest tepee in the village to allow room for the council of elders and other band members to meet while making important decisions. Everyone in camp was expected to be up at dawn. If there had been quarreling or bad feeling in the camp, the chief might call to all the people from outside of his tepee at dawn as they sat around their morning fires. He would remind everyone to be friends and direct them toward what they should do for that day. The elders would call the younger people and tell them to listen, reminding them that "The talk is good." In this way the people started each day with good feelings.

Any chief's power over the individual was limited. He commanded respect only so long as his decisions showed benefit. The

Martin Heyes (standing) and Carl Drake (sitting) have earned the right to wear feathers and fur decorations as very young men. Photo c. 1899. Smithsonian Institution.

elder people would constantly instill in the younger people habits of obedience to the elders and leaders. Obedience was considered a great virtue. This spirit of obedience is what held a group together.

There was no one to enforce a chief's opinion because there was no need to enforce or control. A chief with great ability and authority might take the life of someone who caused him a great deal of trouble, although this was a rare occurrence. The good examples set by elders and leaders made life easy for others. The chief served as mediator when problems arose, counseling on how to do the right thing, to live well, to be good to each other, and "to live straight."

When discussing a leader's role in Ute life, Eddie Box, of the Southern Ute Reservation, says, "In order to become a leader you have to have a real good positive attitude. Leaders were responsible for the development of a man's goodwill by telling the little ones to be what they can be when they grow up. This is what they're responsible for, to teach the young people."

The authority of the chief was limited to his band until it became necessary to negotiate with the white men; at that point, an outstanding leader who was a good mediator gained importance. His authority to speak for the group was subject to limitation by the group's general opinion on any given matter. Long talks over a smoke with the elders and other tribal members would usually help a leader determine the best course to follow.

Leadership was not hereditary. Many times a young man would follow in his father's or grandfather's footsteps because he had acquired leadership abilities by association with good leaders.

The highest authority in the tribe was the council composed of the elders. The chief would preside over meetings with the elders. There was much passing of the pipe and other ceremony associated with these meetings and the decisions made by this group were respected. The Utes had no written laws, no police to enforce their decisions, but relied instead on a moral power and wisdom derived from the elders' years of teachings and spiritual strength.

Ethnologist John Wesley Powell reported:

Aged people are held in a great deal of reverence, though I have known instances of their being treated with much cruelty. Very old women are not found among the Utes. They believe a woman who lives much beyond her period of bearing children will turn into a witch and be doomed to live in a snake-skin. They believe it better to die than meet such a fate. It is quite common for old women to voluntarily starve. I once saw three old women around a fire in a deserted camp, the other members having left sometime before and these remained behind for the purpose of dying. They paid no at-

tention to me but sat gazing into the fire or occasionally rising to
dance a shuffling movement circling around the fire. The dance
was accompanied with a chant for perhaps half an hour. A few days
later, coming to where the tribe were encamped I enquired about
the women and learned they were considered very meritorious.

Shamans and Medicine People

In traditional Ute belief, sickness is not considered to be a state
of the body, rather something that has taken possession of the person. With this theory in mind, it is not surprising that a shaman's
abilities are considered supernatural, obtained not from man but
from the creator.

Shamans and medicine people play an important role in Ute religious life. The position of shaman was confined to men, who gained
their power at an early age through visionary encounters, in which
an animal, bird, or a small dwarf called Pitukupi would reveal the
methods for cures, song and dance patterns, and social rules. The
knowledge needed to carry out the calling of a shaman or medicine
person was gained through a combination of natural ability and interest followed by a lifelong learning process.

When asked how this worked, one Ute medicine woman explained it this way:

> We don't have [concepts] like heaven and hell in our Indian belief.
> We have to learn to accept and overcome negative thoughts and
> make positive ones out of it, to search for understanding. All
> things are good in the creation. Learn to give negative thoughts to
> the grandfathers, they are the only ones who know how to turn it
> around and make it positive. Give bad things in the world to
> grandfather. If your body is sick, talk to the grandfather, give it to
> grandfather. He can turn it around and help you.

The position of a medicine person in the tribe depended upon
their continued ability to cure mental and physical illness and their
ability to reinforce moral values, ideals of gender-appropriate behavior, leadership, and taboos, all important to the serious matter
of survival. At the core of Ute religion is the concept of obtaining
power and guidance from the sun, moon, stars, and plants and animals. A symbol of a person's power source would often decorate
their tepee and clothing. Fetishes or medicine bundles used for curing or protection from illness or for good luck were attached to
clothing or carried in a bag around the neck at all times. Power
must be handled carefully, as it could injure if misused. Those who

abused their power were banned from the group or in some cases killed. Even mentioning that a person was sick or dying could be considered a cause of the illness.

A shaman accepted a certain amount of risk when treating a patient, since revenge might be sought if a patient were to die. Agent James L. Calhoun told of an event in 1852: "Tamouchi the war captain of the Kapotes had a beautiful woman for a wife . . . last week she was taken sick. A doctor belonging to her own band was called in and either the disease, or the medicine was the death of her. Tamouchi paid off the doctor by putting a bullet through him." A similar thing happened when a child died after being treated unsuccessfully by well-known leader Shavano. The child's father shot Shavano outside the agency store in Ouray, Utah. Shavano's son, Charlie, immediately shot his father's killer and his horse and threw both into the river. "Indian justice," reported storekeeper Moulton, who witnessed the incident.

Staying healthy required "thinking good thoughts" and leading a good life. The basic causes of illness were ghosts, witchcraft, violation of taboos, dreams, and intrusive disease-causing objects (such as "little devils") that would enter the body. Things to avoid were the ghosts in whirlwinds, cave dwarfs, coyotes, and evil spirits. Whistling at night was an invitation to an evil spirit to enter your stomach. A fetish for protection from evil spirits was often worn around the neck or fastened to clothing.

Although everyone in the group had a general knowledge of plants used for cures, medicine women were the tribe's pharmacists. They sought to acquire a complete knowledge of herbs and plants used for healing, obtaining powers, and warding away evil spirits. As many as three hundred different plants were used for their therapeutic qualities. Treatments included sage leaves used for colds, split cactus or pine pitch for wounds and sores, a powdered obsidian and sage tea mixture for sore eyes, grass to stop bleeding, and teas from various plants for stomachache.

When a shaman or medicine person was called upon, they were paid with horses, blankets, jewelry, or food. Some shamans specialized in a single sickness. At times the shaman would be called on to travel long distances to visit a patient, or just as often the patient would be taken to visit a shaman who was known to have the right songs and medicine to cure the ailment. A combination of herbal medicine, fasting, sweating, dancing, singing, praying, and blowing or sucking illness from a body were used to rid the patient of the evil spirits causing the sickness.

The Northern Utes were reported to use sweat lodges as early as the 1860s for purposes of curing colds. A vessel filled with hot rocks would be placed between the feet of the patient and a blanket thrown over him. After an hour of more of this cleansing, the patient would sometimes be plunged into cold stream water.

Sweat lodges are used by many Utes today. The lodges are usually small domed structures that will hold several people. They are built in a certain pattern of curved boughs forming a half circle that is covered with hides or blankets. A pit is dug in the middle of the floor to hold volcanic rock that has been heated outside the lodge. The rock is arranged in ceremonial fashion, aligned to the four directions, before the entrance to the lodge is closed and the seated participants are surrounded by darkness. Offerings of sage and sometimes smoke are made to Mother Earth and to the grandfathers. Water is carefully poured on the hot rock and the steam and chanting of songs surround the senses and the body. Sweat lodge ceremonies are held for many purposes, the most common being healing, celebrations, prayer, and the cleansing of body, mind, and spirit in preparation for other events important to the Ute way of life.

Medicine men were still practicing on the Southern Ute reservation in the 1920s. "The custom of calling for the Indian medicine man is being discouraged and every effort is being made to influence them to abandon this habit. Oftentimes the Indians come to the office and request me to pay the bills of these medicine men," reported Agency Superintendent E.E. McKean.

A Ute elder recalled the days of the old Indian doctors, and mourned their passing: "That was a long time ago. There's no more of them now, none at all. These generations haven't got it, the knowledge wasn't passed on to them."

Religion, Song, and Dance

"We should be respectful of religion," says Ute elder Annabelle Eagle.

Indians never had a word for evil. That was a force that was not acknowledged, only disharmony. Living in harmony with our fellow men, with nature and with our creator is the ultimate goal of life on earth. The word evil and its connotation came with the white man and his religion. People only concentrated on bringing forth a force or a goodness to overcome a deficiency in one's life. Then truly we reach the happy hunting grounds! Even if you call yourself a twentieth century Indian, a paper Indian [a cardholding tribal member who lives away from the reservation], an apple [a pejora-

Getting ready for the powwow, c. 1902. H.H. Tammen photo, Smithsonian Institution.

tive term: "red on the outside, white on the inside"], or whatever, these teaching apply to all of us. To know is to understand.

Religion, song, and dance are inseparable in Ute life. They have always been as much a part of everyday life as food and water. Dances were held for both social and religious purposes. A variety of musical instruments accompany the many types of dances and ceremonies.

Hand drums used in social dances and big double-headed drums used for the Sun Dance are late adoptions. Water drums, made by stretching buckskin across a pottery bowl or crock, or in later times an iron kettle, were used at scalp dances, for parades, and more recently, at peyote meetings. One-hole whistles and gourd and hoof rattles of antelope or deer dewclaws had multiple uses. The six-holed wooden courting flute was considered a sure form of "love magic" if a man could lure his sweetheart to the place where he played. Each man composed his own melody to call his true love to him. Flutes were often passed down from father to son. Older instruments include the rasp and bone used in the Bear Dance.

The Circle Dance, War Dance, Shield Dance, Dog Dance, Tea Dance, Lame Dance, Double Dance, Square Dance, and Coyote Dance were all of a social nature. A large gathering of neighboring tribes, friends, and relatives marked the important annual Bear

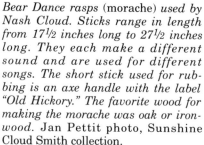

Bear Dance rasps (morache) *used by Nash Cloud. Sticks range in length from 17½ inches long to 27½ inches long. They each make a different sound and are used for different songs. The short stick used for rubbing is an axe handle with the label "Old Hickory." The favorite wood for making the morache was oak or ironwood.* Jan Pettit photo, Sunshine Cloud Smith collection.

Courting flutes were made from carefully selected red cedar. The wood was split in two, the center was hollowed out, and the two halves were put back together with cedar gum and the flute was wrapped with thongs. Often the flutes were decorated with paintings or carvings, such as the animal on this one. Center of Southwest Studies, Fort Lewis College.

Dance and Sun Dance. This socializing is an opportunity for feasts, games, family visits, and meetings with other tribes and neighbors to discuss family and tribal problems.

Ruxton witnessed a Scalp Dance in 1847 and recorded his observations in his diary. When the Ute men returned with scalps, they were hung on a single pole in front of the medicine man's tepee. Ruxton described the medicine men as attired in skins of wolves and bears and bearing long, peeled wands of cherry in their hands. Next to a small fire outside the medicine man's tepee was the scalp pole, next to which one medicine man sat with a drum between his knees that he tapped at intervals with his hand, "eliciting from the instrument a hollow monotonous sound." The braves and warriors squatted around the fire in two circles, those engaged in the expedition being in the inner circle.

Bear Dance music is made by rubbing rasps (woni'thonkunaps), *which resemble giant jaw bones, with deer shin bones. The rasps rest on a metal or wooden resonance chamber covered with rawhide. Older-style resonators were made by covering a hole dug in the ground or a hollow log with rawhide. The music rumbles through the earth, awakening the bears and the land.* L.C. Thorne collection, Thorne Studio.

Squaws in robes of whitely dressed buckskins, garnished with beads and porcupine quills, their faces painted bright red and black . . . ranged themselves round the outside of the square. A bevy of women, shoulder to shoulder, then advanced from the four sides of the square, some shaking a rattle-drum in time with their steps, commenced a jumping, jerking dance, now lifting one foot from the ground, now rising with both, accompanying the dance with a low chant, which swelled from a low whisper to the utmost extent of their voices—now dying away, and again bursting into vociferous measure . . . six squaws, with their faces painted a deadened black made their appearance from the crowd, and in a soft and sweet measure, chanted a lament for the braves the nation had lost in the late battle. Soon as they drew near the scalp-pole, their melancholy note changed to the music of gratified revenge. In a series of jumps, raising the feet alternately but a little distance from the ground, they made their way, through an interval left in the circle of warriors to the grim pole . . . and encircling it in perfect silence for a few moments.

The black-faced women burst forth with songs telling of the achievement of their victorious braves. They addressed the scalps as "sisters" (to be called a woman is the greatest insult that could be offered), spit at them, and lashed verbal insults at them for daring to come to a country where the warriors and young men despised them.

While all this was happening, "the boys and children of all ages, mounted on bareback horses, [were] galloping and screaming round and round, with all the eagerness of excitement and curiosity."

The Taviwach, Yampa, and Uintah Utes joined the Fort Hall Shoshone and Bannock Indians to participate in the Ghost Dance religion in 1870. The dance promised a solution to the problems facing all Indians at a time when they were miserable and confused about their place in the rapidly changing world around them. The dance was revealed to a visionary with the message that faithful adherence to the dance would rid the world of whites, restore Indian land, and resurrect dead Indians. After joining in the dancing for two years they apparently stopped ghost dancing.

Sun Dance

The Sun Dance, according to Joseph Jorgensen in the book *The Sun Dance Religion*, is a post-reservation phenomenon that began about 1890 for Northern Utes, 1900 for Ute Mountain Utes, and 1904 for Southern Utes. "The focus of the Sun Dance was changed from ensuring successful bison hunts and warfare to an increasing concern over illness and community misery." Ute elders say the basis for the dance is much older.

Sun Dance corral under construction at White Rocks, c. 1900. Everything about the corral and the men, who dance without food or water for three to four days, has a symbolic significance. The center pole is said to represent the creator or center of power, white and blue flags attached to the pole represent the sun and sky, the colors painted on each pole and on the dancers, as well as the eagle bone whistles blown by the dancers, mean individual things to each man. L.C. Thorne collection, Thorne Studio.

Commissioner of Indian Affairs Cato Sells ordered every Ute reservation superintendent and agent to "Prohibit the Sun Dance or any dance of a similar nature." In a 1914 telegram, he demanded that the dance be stopped at the Uintah-Ouray Reservation, stating, "This dance is a great detriment to moral and industrial interest of the Indians and cannot be allowed." Some citizens of Vernal, Utah, could see no harm in the Sun Dance. People came for miles around to witness the event. It was good for business. The Salt Lake City newspaper carried an editorial in favor of the dance, saying "Dancing was originally an art employed in the service of religion, used for purposes of worship, and it is only then that art comes to its right." Mr. Sells did not agree, warning the people of Vernal not to encourage the dance. "I do not wish to subject your community to the indignity of sending troops," he wrote.

When Sells was notified that the dance had started he called upon the United States marshal to stop it. The marshal responded by traveling immediately to Vernal (a three-day trip). He reported to Sells shortly after his arrival. "The Sun Dance, which I was directed to use all lawful means to prevent, had already taken place

Each year Duard and Esther Campbell, who lived in Vernal, Utah, would take meat to the Sun Dance for their Ute friends, the Atwines. In return they were given one of these small beaded ornaments each year they attended. The buffalo head is made from a sheep vertebra and rooster spurs. Campbell collection, Museum of Western Colorado.

on Lake Fork, about thirty miles northwest of the town of Myton. There were about eight male Indians who were active participants in the ceremony which was witnessed by about three hundred Indian of both sexes," he reported. "My information was that there were no ill effects from the dance. The old idea of testing the ability to endure pain to initiate the subject into the band of warriors having been eliminated, the idea of its affording curative effects being now most prominent."

On the Southern Ute Reservation, Superintendent McKean was reprimanded for allowing the Sun Dance to be held. McKean reported that the dance was held without his permission, although he did observe it. He reported:

> It was conducted orderly and no barbarous or immoral practice was engaged in. The dance was held about two miles from the agency and but a few rods from the public road in an open field. The dance lodge was constructed from boughs and opened on the east side. The dancers were clothed from the waist nearly to the knees, a fuller costume than is often worn by athletes in public contest. Each dancer had a whistle which he blew continually. The dance consisted simply of running backwards and forwards to a pole, each dancer having his individual path. There were no strings, or cords attached to the pole nor to the dancers, they were not whipped and there were none of the old time features of a sun dance. Strict order and quiet maintained. One of the Indians reminded some of the white spectators that they did not wish them to laugh or talk, but to keep quiet and respectful. Eleven Indians took part. All good farmers. In no cases did the stock or work of the Indians who took part in the dancing suffer from neglect. I am of the opinion that it is not harmful. I realize fully that it does not have a christianizing effect upon these Indians, but I do believe that it does not have any immoral effect upon them.

Despite Sells' objections, the Sun Dance continued. One thing is for certain: the dance has gained importance since the 1890s. In the middle of summer, a man accepted by his people as the Sun Dance chief selects a time, place, and length for the dance. The original version began with a mock battle followed by the erection of an elaborate dance corral. To the beat of the drum, the rhythm of the singers, and encouragement from bystanders, the dancers shuffled to and from a center pole for three days and nights or longer. The dancers went without food or water, and took only short rests. The dance is a curing ritual with great emphasis on the individual's seeking to acquire power from the creator, in the belief that a good performance brings general good health and welfare to the community.

Bear Dance — *mama-kwa-nhkap*

The oldest ceremony the Ute people have is the Bear Dance. The dance is held each year on the three Ute reservations. When the bears "wake up," it is time to visit relatives, play games, to mourn those who are gone, and to welcome new members of the tribe.

The Bear Dance leader begins making plans for the three- to four-day dance when the first spring thunder is heard. The men make the plans and do all the preparation for the dance and the feast that follows to honor the women.

The dance is held in a large circular brush corral of cedar trees gathered every year by the men. The corral entrance faces the ris-

The Cat Man (moose-a-la-pete-ah) in the foreground keeps order while the dance is on, making sure the line stays straight, and cutting away the partners for the last dances. He often brings roars of laughter from the spectators when he uses his stick to lightly tap a dancer that gets out of line. The elaborate horsehair and beadwork hairpiece is typical of the Cat Man, who is usually the most decorated man at the Bear Dance. L.C. Thorne collection, Thorne Studio.

The Bear appears! During the last day of Bear Dance, couples have been paired off to dance together. Suddenly, the dancing ceases and dancers dressed as a male and female bear spring into the circle, pawing and prancing to symbolize that the prayers have been heard and the earth is awakened. L.C. Thorne collection, Thorne Studio.

ing sun in the east. Two cedar trees are positioned on either side of the entrance just inside the circle. Men sit on the north side of the circle, women on the south side. The singers sit under a brush shelter at the west side of the corral with their long metal resonator and their notched sticks that make a noise like a bear growling or thunder rumbling.

When the singers play a "choose your partners" song, the women walk to the men's side of the circle, and each woman waves her shawl toward the man she wishes to dance with and walks back to the center of the corral. There the women form a line facing the singers. Women are not supposed to choose their husbands or any relatives to dance with. The music stops for a few minutes while the "Cat Man" (moose-a-la-pete-ah), equipped with a long stick, encourages the men to get up and dance. The men form a line facing the women. When the music begins, the women begin with two steps forward and three steps back. The men move forward and the women move back. The line is almost like a wave moving back and forth in perfect unison.

The Cat Man keeps everyone in line, making sure no one is out of step and that the men and women don't touch or bump into each other while they are in lines. Each day more dancers join the group and each dance lasts longer and longer.

Traditionally, on the last day of the dance, the Cat Man would separate dancers into couples by "cutting them up" (separating them by placing the pole along the side of a man and woman dancer facing each other) and the couple would dance in a kind of jogging step back and forth with the woman always facing the dancers and the men facing the east. The couple's dance is almost a friendly contest of endurance between the men and women. As evening approaches on the last day the music never ceases until someone falls.

As the dancers leave the circle they leave tobacco, a piece of cloth, a feather, or something on the cedar tree symbolizing leaving their problems or a family member's problems or sickness, so that they can start a new life and a new year.

Everyone gathers for a feast held for all who attended the dance. For everyone who attended the 1984 Bear Dance at the Southern Ute Reservation, five hundred pounds of beef, cooked into a stew, was served from huge pots, accompanied by corn on the cob, rolls, and thick slices of watermelon.

Bear Dance Time
by Annabelle W. Eagle
Southern Ute Drum, Spring 1987

A time for a new beginning, the starting of new friendships and renewal of old friendships. A time of remembrance of long ago days, and long ago friends and relatives. A time of giving thanks to the Creator for the time of survival during the harsh and cold winters. The Ute People join with all nature in celebration of the renewal of life and its meanings. It is known that each person, animal, and plant awakens and starts their regrowth in their given time.

At this time, the Ute People will dance with celebration of the start of spring. Long ago, this way of celebration was given to the Ute People by their brother and protector, the Bear.

The songs and the dance, methods of building the brush corral, and the making and use of instruments, all were given them. These instruments are the resonator, the bear notched growler stick and the rubbing stick. The resonator is placed over a pit, dug in the ground. Rubbing the two sticks together produces the growl and scratching sound of the bear as he sharpens his claws for his coming hunts.

The dance is in imitation of the bear as he steps forward and backward with each thrust at a standing tree. Altogether, this cre-

*ates a rhythm which quickens the flow of blood in the body and re-
news the zest for life. The singing begins.*

*It is through this special tie with nature, which makes our Ute
People who they are and why they survive in an ever-changing
world. With the hustle and bustle of readying the grounds, the
building of the brush corral, comes a feeling of primitive urges our
forefathers must have felt, when they too hustled and bustled about.*

*New and old songs are sung in practice. Clothing is made and
repaired to be worn. Extra food is bought and stored in anticipa-
tion of having visitors. Advice and instructions are given to those
who will be this year's crop of new dancers. Instructions on whom
not to dance with and to stay in line with other dancers. Advice to
maintain proper decorum and to be on one's best behavior to one
and all. To sit on the proper side of the corral. Advice to have a
partner who will relieve you, when the last long big dance begins.
To listen to and respect the Cat Man with the big stick. This is advice to the young men who tend to run away.*

*Long ago, no hats or blankets were worn when dancing, but
today it is allowed, because the hat and the shawl have become a
part of the costume to be worn during dancing.*

*We feel very fortunate that we still have the Bear Dance in our
tribe. People from other tribes come and enjoy taking part in our
festivities because it is a great time for all. The feast prepared by
the tribe ends this year's dance.*

*So, amid laughter and fond farewells, we all go our different
ways to live out the coming year.*

Stories Told at Night

Storytelling and winter seemed to go together. According to Ute
elder Guy Pinnecoose, "Old men would sit up all night in winter-
time and tell stories about everything that happened in their lives
and animals and things like that." Even if you were from another
tribe and couldn't speak the language, a story told by a low campfire would be understood, as the storyteller's skill communicated
his message by a strange look in the eye or a facial gesture combined with skillful hand and body motions. The people listened and
observed, alternately laughing or sitting spellbound as the storyteller impresses a moral, implants a proverb, or teaches a lesson to
the young.

Stories often hid a moral that was acted out by animals to replace
human characters. Old Coyote was a favorite. He was a devil or
hero who dealt with the basic problems facing the Ute people. One
story finds Old Coyote making fun of Porcupine for wanting to ride
a buffalo. Porcupine learns to ride the buffalo by holding onto his

horns and they have a race with Old Coyote on a horse and Porcupine on his buffalo. Porcupine wins.

Winter and nighttime were the proper times for storytelling. Telling stories helped to while away the long hours when people were confined in small quarters. Some stories take only minutes, others take hours or several nights to tell. There are many types of stories. Tales could explain the culture, hunting practices, and religious beliefs. Tales told to children often conveyed morals, ethics, taboos, and traditional lessons that would keep them safe. There are tales and entertaining stories told for fun, in which animals are representatives of humans and are ridiculed.

This story is one Major John Wesley Powell collected before beginning his famous 1869 Colorado Scientific Exploring Expedition. He and nine other men were likely the first to navigate the raging Colorado River.

The Origin of the Canyons of the Colorado

Many ages ago when wise and good men lived on the earth, the great Chief of all the Utes lost his beloved wife. Day and night he grieved, and all his people were sad. Then Ta-vwoats appeared to the chief and tried to comfort him, but his sorrow could not be allayed. So at last Ta-vwoats promised to take him to a country away to the southwest where he said his dead wife had gone and let him see how happy she was if he would agree to grieve no more on his return. So he promised.

Then Ta-vwoats took his magical ball and rolled it before him, and as it rolled it rent the earth and mountains, and crushed the rocks and made a way for them to that beautiful land—a trail through the mountains which intervene between that home of the dead and the hunting ground of the living. And following the ball, which was a rolling globe of fire, they came at last to the Spirit Land. Then the great Chief saw his wife and the blessed abode of the Spirits where all was plenty and all was joy, and he was glad.

Now when they had returned Ta-vwoats enjoined upon the chief that he should never travel this trail again during life, and that all his people should be warned not to walk therein. Yet still he feared that they would attempt it so he rolled a river into the trail—a mad raging river into the gorge made by the globe of fire, which should overwhelm any who might seek to enter there.

Games

The Ute people love games. During the day men, women, and children might play games but never together. They enjoyed 16 stick dice, 4 stick dice, archery, arrow tossing, ring spearing, juggling clay balls, cat's cradle, rock throwing called "Quoits," tossing a circle of willow (similar to a Frisbee), foot racing, wrestling, and other games of skill. Hand games were often accompanied by singing. After the Utes were moved to reservations, card games and gambling became even more popular to fill the idle hours.

A traditional Ute hand game was the stick game. Ute elder Sunshine Smith describes the game:

> There are three parts: sticks like cards, counting sticks, and the round rock. You have to find a round rock, which is hard to find. There is a hole drilled out in the bottom. Everyone puts their bet under the rock where the hole is. The card sticks are held in the hand and dropped on the top of the rock. The number of lines showing on the fallen sticks is the count. You take a counter to keep track of your lines. We grew up playing this. All night long we used to play it. A whole bunch of us were playing. We'd say, I'll bet my horse, I'll bet my dog, or saddle, our clothes, and pretty soon one person has it all.

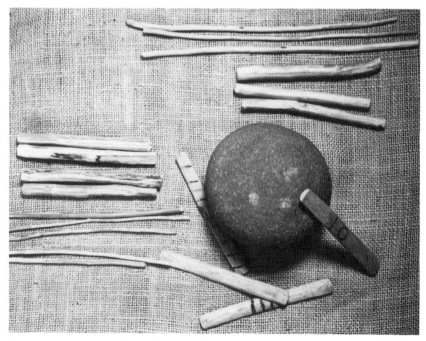

Equipment used for the stick game. "My mother or father made this, I guess. I've had it a long time," says Ute elder Sunshine Cloud Smith. Jan Pettit photo, Sunshine Smith collection.

Horse racing has always been a favorite sport among the men. Only two horses were entered in a race, but several heats might be required before the spectators would agree on who owned the best horse. Trickery and shrewdness were as much a part of the sport as the betting, much to the dismay of one party of sportsmen near Caribou, Colorado. Chief Antelope arrived with three squaws riding his best trained running ponies and began ridiculing the white men's horses, claiming any of his "squaws' ponies" could beat them easily. The white men, knowing that an Indian would never let a woman ride his race horses, fell into the trap and proceeded to bet their hunting outfits on a race. The embarrassed sportsmen lost their entire outfit and were forced to walk back to town with nothing left but the clothes on their backs.

Shinney, an ancient Ute game similar to field hockey, is played by teams of women on a field about 250 feet long. The object of the game is to get the four-inch ball, made of buckskin stuffed with deer hair, over the line at the opponents' end. Usually the ball is hit with the curved wooden shinney sticks, although kicking the ball, grabbing other players' sticks, and tripping are all allowed. L.C. Thorne collection, Thorne Studio.

Gambling with cards or hand games made from wood or bones filled many idle hours after the Utes were placed on reservations. The flash in the middle of the circle of men is from a mirror. Shining a mirror at a photographer was thought to keep the photographer from taking your spirit. L.C. Thorne collection, Thorne Studio.

The Utes watched closely the "crazy white men" who dug up rocks and hauled them away. They didn't mind them taking the gold and silver as long as they didn't build houses and stay in Ute country. Caricature from Harpers Weekly Gazette.

Chapter 5
Cultures in Conflict

Spanish policy, trade conditions, or aggression on the part of other tribes would result in the Utes alternately being allies or enemies of the Spanish, Navajo, and Comanche. When it would benefit them, the Utes would join forces with one or the other. Spanish and Indian relationships in New Mexico during the late 1600s and early 1700s were generally of benefit to both peoples.

Spanish governors sponsored yearly fairs near Taos, New Mexico, where all Indians could come to trade. A truce was made during fair time by all the Indians who attended. The governor might not have had problems with the Indians during the trading fairs, but he did have to keep a close eye on unscrupulous traders and settlers who might cheat the Indians and rile them into a desire for revenge on Spanish settlements at a later date. Sevor Don Pedro Tamaron described the fair in 1760:

> The governor with a great part of his presidio and people come to those fairs, which they (Indians) call ransoms. They bring captives to sell, buckskins, many buffalo hides, and booty that they have taken in other parts—horses, guns, muskets, ammunition, knives, meat, and various other things. No money circulates in these fairs but articles are traded for each other and in this way those people provide themselves.

The Utes brought raw materials, tanned buffalo, deer, and elk hides (described as dressed delicately fine), fresh meat, furs, and basketry for trade. They traded with the Spanish for axes, bridles, knives, and trinkets.

The Navajo wove blankets with bold black and red or yellow patterns called the "chief blanket" that were traded almost exclusively with the Utes. According to Hildegard Wetherill, wife of a well-

known trader, "The Navajos traded chief blankets for Ute buckskins and baskets. The Utes did not weave. The Navajos stopped
making (baskets) years before. The Navajos wanted only their own
pattern in baskets and the Utes wanted their own pattern in blankets, with slight variations to tell them apart. The blankets were
made for tall or short men by order and were of such a fine weave
as to make them pliable for a garment." A blanket was worth about
five tanned buckskins or one well-dressed buffalo robe or one good
mare.

Trading for furs became of less interest to white traders with the
increase in the illegal trade in the more valuable Indian captives
and children, who could be sold to the Spaniards for great profit. At
that time, a large antelope skin or buckskin was worth two pesos
each. Small antelope skins were valued at two for one peso. A horse
was worth three pesos. A saddle, bridle, stirrups, and spurs for one
horseman brought twelve pesos. A month's salary for a common soldier was fifteen pesos. One peso a day was all a working man might
make. With such a table of values, a slave woman was worth eight
horses, thirteen buckskins, or two months' labor by a soldier. No
wonder that slaves were a valuable and much sought-after trade
item.

Most Indian slaves were put to work on farms. They learned a
great deal about civilized life, including the care, training, and
value of the horse. Although the Utes acquired a few horses during
the early 1600s by raiding and trading, the horse had made no noticeable impact on their lifestyle until the Pueblo Indians' revolt
against the Spaniards in 1680. Whether the Utes helped in this revolt is not certain. Numerous Ute slaves were freed and herds of
horses belonging to the Spanish became the property of the Ute Indians at this time.

The Spanish demand for illegal trade in slaves was to cause
many problems for the Utes. The Utes were becoming quite a problem for their Indian and Spanish neighbors by the 1700s. Utes
began raiding weaker tribes, particularly the Paiutes, who at times
would trade their children for much-needed food and supplies. The
Utes seldom killed while raiding. They preferred to take what they
wanted and make a quick getaway. Standing fights were avoided.
Obtaining plunder was more important than the prestige won by
rash displays of valor. They would continue raiding the Pueblo Indians and Spanish settlements in Arizona and New Mexico for the
next hundred years.

Ethnologist Ann Smith reported a story of a brave Ute warrior
who found a Comanche camp: "One man was lying asleep with his

grazing horse held by a rope in his hand. The Ute was so brave, he slipped over by that sleeping man, took the rope, cut it, and stole the horse. The man did not wake up."

In 1846, George Frederick Ruxton traveled through Mexican settlements in New Mexico on his way to the Rocky Mountains to hunt. He was appalled at the misery and degradation of the Mexican people living on the Rio Colorado. "Growing a bare sufficiency for their own support, they hold the little land they cultivate, and their wretched hovels, on sufferance from the barbarous Yutas, who actually tolerate their presence in their country for the sole purpose of having at their command a stock of grain and a herd of mules and horses, which they make no scruple of helping themselves to." At times, the Utes made life so miserable for small settlements that the entire town would relocate rather than endure another raid. In 1826, Manuel Gregario Torres of Abiquiu wrote to the governor complaining that the Yutas who visit constantly were eating him out of house and home. "What can I do? I am poor, and need aid to feed them."

A Ute man laughed when telling this story, "The Pueblo Indians planned for the Utes' raids. It was kind of like a game. They used to raise enough corn to eat, enough to plant new crops the next year, and enough for the Utes to steal."

The most notorious of all raiders was Chief Walkara and his brother Arrapeen, possibly aided by mountain men Pegleg Smith and Joe Walker. Their raiding and horse-stealing ring reached as far as California and resulted in hundreds of horses for the Utah Utes. The Utes' ability to withdraw into the mountains always gave them an advantage that few could surpass.

At times, soldiers were stationed at Taos or Santa Fe to subdue the "Yutas" and discourage their attacks on surrounding pueblos. In 1719, the governor of New Mexico mustered his troops and called for volunteers to retaliate against the Utes' increasing raids on settlements. About eight hundred soldiers, settlers, and Indians trailed the Utes for over a month through the mountains. Near Dillon, Colorado, they encountered their most vicious enemy, poison ivy. Sick and discouraged, they gave up the chase.

Troubles and Treaties

The Utes were at the height of their Tepee Culture by 1840. The next fifty years would bring disastrous changes in their lives.

The changes began so slowly they were hardly noticeable at first. During the early 1800s, trappers and traders began living among the Ute people. The trade goods they brought were welcome additions to the Utes' lives. The trapper and trader lifestyle was similar to that of the Indians. They usually got along well, but there were exceptions. In the winter of 1823–24, Etienne Provost was trapping near the Utah city that bears his name when several of his party were killed by Indians he called Snakes but were probably Utes.

Following the war between the United States and Mexico, a rapid infusion of Anglos settled in the Southwest. In the period between 1598 and 1848, when either Spain or Mexico claimed ownership of the Southwest, many land grants were given to Spanish or Mexican citizens in southern Colorado and northern New Mexico. These lands were traditionally areas occupied by the Utes. The United States agreed to honor these grants by terms made in the Treaty of Guadalupe Hidalgo (1848), which ended the war with Mexico. These lands were claimed without any treaty with the Utes.

By this time the Spanish had attempted several unsuccessful campaigns to remove the Utes from this area and to stop their raiding. As more settlers moved into southern Colorado, raiding increased. In order to stop these raids, Lucien Maxwell (owner of the Maxwell grant in the San Luis Valley) and Antonine Lerous joined Spanish soldiers and their Indian allies and marched on the Utes. They surrounded a camp and attacked, killing many and destroying the scarce supplies and shelters. In retaliation, the Utes killed the next group of Anglos they met, including mountain man Bill Williams, who was married to a Ute woman. When they realized they had killed their good friend, they took his body to their village and gave him a chief's burial and grieved for him as if they had lost one of their own leaders.

The first peace treaty with the United States was signed at Abiquiu, New Mexico, in 1849, by a small group of the Ute people. This was the beginning of a long series of treaties, bribes, threats, and promises, which often resulted in the United States taking what land it wanted regardless of agreements with the Indians.

Fort Massachusetts, near the present town of Fort Garland, Colorado, was established in 1852 as the first military fort in Colorado. The fort was to provide protection for settlers in southern Colorado. More and more settlers moved into the area around the fort, resulting in the ultimate destruction of the native resources.

The Utes always objected to settlers who moved in and built permanent structures. In one instance a settler named Lamb drove a bunch of Texas steers to an area where he planned to settle on the eastern slope of the Colorado Rockies. He named the area Texas Creek after a group of his steers were spooked by a mountain lion.

Rare photo taken of the Utes at the Abiquiu, New Mexico, Agency, c. 1850. The man with the sword could be Kaniache, the famous Moache chief who signed the first peace treaty with the United States in 1849. He and two other Ute warriors joined the Union Army to fight beside their friend and agent Kit Carson at the Battle of Adobe Walls. He visited Washington in 1868, where he spoke against the Brunot agreement of 1873, the last treaty he was to sign. Warnky and Abbott photo, Museum of New Mexico.

Even though Lamb had been there long enough to make friends with Ute leader Colorow, he was told firmly by the Indians that he couldn't build a cabin there, only a tepee.

Settlements were invariably located in areas close to resources and water used by the Indians. The newcomers depended upon many of the same resources. Wild game previously hunted by the Indians provided the settlers fresh meat, traditional Indian root-digging grounds were tilled or fenced for pastures. Streams and rivers where the Indians had gathered berries and camped were lined with settlers' farms. The Utes simply took from the settlers what they needed to replace whatever native resources were missing. The settlers retaliated by killing and so did the Utes. The Utes tried everything—scare tactics, threatening, raiding, and burning—to rid themselves of the settlers. Nothing worked.

Agencies

Agencies were established in New Mexico in the early 1850s to distribute goods promised in treaties and to account for the Indians' welfare and whereabouts. Among the agents and superintendents responsible for Indian affairs were those whose jobs were a result of a political or religious appointment. These appointees, no matter how conscientious they were, usually had little or no understanding of the Ute people and often had little concern for their problems. Many showed a dislike for dealing with the Indians at all. Even when an appropriate agent or superintendent was assigned to a job, government policy and red tape often hindered their objectives. Agent Norton wrote:

> I regret that I am to be cursed and overrun by a daily increasing throng of filthy, lousy, naked, and starving Indians crying for food for themselves and their little ones without the authority or ability to alleviate their suffering. I regret that I am thus compelled to submit to such torture and make a martyr of myself simply because the Department has not sufficient confidence in my integrity and judgment.

Those Indians that rebelled and raided for their food and supplies invariably received more supplies faster in the interest of pacifying them. Peaceful Indians could not understand this system by which troublemakers received rewards—maybe it was better to cause a little trouble and receive some gifts.

Ute leaders were invited to a peace conference in 1854 at Taos, New Mexico, where Christopher "Kit" Carson was the Indian agent. Gifts of blanket coats were given to Ute leaders. Every leader who received a coat contracted smallpox. The Indians felt this was a deliberate attempt to kill them and they joined with the Apaches to drive the settlers from their country. Some elder Utes still feel this germ warfare was deliberate. Deliberate or not, it started a war that resulted in the deaths of many settlers and Indians.

Dick Wootton, mountain man, rancher, freighter, road builder, and long-time friend of the Utes, warned the seventeen Mexican trappers and traders at Fort Pueblo that the Indians were raiding and on the warpath. Since these people had never had any problems with the usually friendly Utes before, they refused to listen. On Christmas Day, 1854, a group of Moache Utes under the leadership of Chief Tierra Blanca was allowed inside the fort for a friendly smoke. In the midst of the festivities the Utes attacked, killing all but one man and taking the only woman at the fort and her two children captive. The man reached the safety of a nearby ranch where he died from his wounds. The two boys were rescued but their mother had been killed within a few days "because she cried too much."

The Utes continued raiding in the Arkansas Valley area until their long-time enemies, the Arapaho, attacked while the Utes were off-guard during a victory celebration near Canon City, Colorado. As part of their loot, the Arapaho took the disease-ridden blanket coats. Many of them also died from smallpox.

Indian Agent Kit Carson was determined to control "his" Indians. Feeling it was "his duty" he joined an army expedition against the Utah Utes and Apache Indians in 1855. The following is a condensed version of a very long and detailed description sent to the commissioner of Indian Affairs by Carson. Note that the Utes typically disappeared into the mountains at first contact with the intruders.

> Colonel Fauntleroy and Four companies of mounted volunteers, one company of artillery, two companies of soldiers and one company of spies marched from Don Fernandez de Taos, New Mexico to Fort Massachusetts. [They continued with] thirty days provisions and half forage for four hundred animals all packed on mules . . . after five days we reached Sah-wach Pass about one hundred and twenty miles from Fort Mass. where we found about one hundred lodges of Utah and Apache Indians . . . having espied us . . . they immediately sent off all their stock and families and the warriors remained to give us battle . . . the bravery and unerring aim of the troops soon put the Indians to flight. [The Utahs and Apaches went separate ways with the troops following the Apaches.] On through Punche Pass . . . we discovered three Utahs . . . and succeeded in killing one and taking one prisoner. [The troops followed a trail and] found where 75 or 80 lodges had encamped a short time before . . . We ascertained they had separated into parties or bands . . . We followed the largest trail over high and rugged mountains until the spies took an Apache woman and child prisoner and captured eight horses. [The Apache woman told them Chacon was their leader and seven Indians had been killed.] Arriving near the river we discovered the Indians. A charge was ordered . . . the troops went manfully to work and soon routed the Apaches, capturing about fifty head of horses and mules . . . from the large amount of mule meat captured I would judge that the Apaches must be in a very destitute and starving condition . . . Our provision nearly out we gave up the chase and returned through the Wet Mountain Valley and Moscos Pass to Fort Massachusetts . . . Very few of the campaigns that have been made against these Indians have proven so successful or taught the Indians the force of our arms as the one made by Colonel Fauntleroy.

Colonel Christopher "Kit" Carson, Commander of the 1st New Mexico Volunteer Cavalry Regiment. This 1864 photograph may be the first photograph ever taken of the famous scout, mountain man, and Indian agent. He, like the Indians of his era, disliked and avoided having his picture taken. Museum of New Mexico.

Kit Carson continued leading groups of soldiers against the Utes and Apaches until the thoroughly defeated Indians wandered into the agency starving, homeless, and ready to sign a treaty in order to obtain much-needed supplies.

The government assigned official representatives to negotiate treaties. The Indians were given presents to show the good faith of the government, and bargains were sealed with smokes and hand-shakes. When Governor John Evans held a peace council with the Utes at Fort Garland in the San Luis Valley in 1865, he took along "thirteen wagons heavily laden with gifts for the Indians. One wagon was loaded with navy tobacco, the plugs being a foot in length."

The Indians assumed when they signed a treaty that a bargain was made on both sides. They thought the "Great White Father" in Washington had also made a bargain to deliver food, supplies, and tools right away, as promised. Government red tape didn't work that way. Some treaties were never ratified by the government. This meant that the Indians never received what they had been promised, nor were they notified that the government did not in-tend to keep its side of the bargain. The Indian agents were left to deal with the hungry and unhappy Indians with no resources to solve the problems. At times incompetence and downright fraud

The Ute Chief with Agent (possibly Lafayette Head) and Col. Berr. One of many photographs that offers a challenging research project. The majority of the photographs at the Smithsonian Institution were turned over to the institution when various government offices were closed or moved to other divisions. Few photographs are identified with either dates, locations, or identities of the persons in the photographs. Smithsonian Institution.

prevailed in one or more steps of delivering goods. Sometimes more than a year would pass before the Indians received promised gifts and supplies. A year is a long time to wait when there is no longer food available except at the homes of settlers who live on lands that had always supplied the Utes with food.

It is doubtful that the Ute people realized that they were giving away their right to occupy their lands by signing treaties. Justice Black in a 1945 case, *U.S. v. Shoshone*, stated: "Ownership meant no more to them than to roam the land as a great common, and to possess and enjoy it in the same way that they possessed and enjoyed the sunlight and the west wind and the feel of spring in the air. Acquisitiveness, which develops a law of real property, is an accomplishment of the 'civilized.'"

Mormon Policy

By the 1850s, the ancient homelands of the Utah Utes around Sevier Lake and Salt Lake in Utah became the sacred home of the
Latter Day Saints. Brigham Young, Mormon leader and ex-officio
commissioner of Indian Affairs, said he was making an attempt to
treat the Indian fairly. His values were still the same as other nineteenth century settlers: if the land was not being used to maximum
benefit by their standards, it was all right to take it for the best
use. If the Indians wanted to farm and use the land in a "civilized"
manner, they could stay.

Young started farm projects in several areas where the Utes
could learn the white man's ways. He had an unusual policy toward
the Indians, whom he felt were the "seeds of Abraham" referred to
in his Book of Mormon. His contradictory messages had a double
edge. "Feed the Indians, for it is cheaper to feed them than to fight
them. Treat them kindly, and trust them as Indians, and not as
your equals. Never let them come into your houses . . . treat the Indians kindly, now is the time for you to finish your forts and make
them doubly strong." Indian oral traditions relate horrible mass
killings of men, women, and children who were enticed into Mormon buildings or driven into lakes to drown.

Brigham Young wrote to the commissioner of Indian Affairs in
Washington, c. 1854, concerning problems caused by travelers en
route to California. He suggested that, "Peaceful relations with the
Indians be interposed on behalf of travelers . . . Indians have had a
most flagrant and savage feeling of vengeance because of the practice of indiscriminately shooting and poisoning them." The killing of
Captain John W. Gunnison and seven of his survey party near Sevier Lake in Utah in 1853 was an act of retaliation for foolish con-
duct by emigrants.

Problems between the United States government and the Mormons ultimately resulted in hardships and starvation for the Utes.
In 1865, Brigham Young advised the Utah Utes to sign a treaty giving up their claim to all of Utah Territory except the Uintah Valley
in exchange for $900,000 to be paid to them over the next 60 years.
The Indians would be allowed to fish in accustomed places and to
gather roots and berries, and were to be provided schools, supplies,
and "allotments." Chief Soweett explained that they, "did not want
to sell their land and go away; they wanted to live around the
graves of their fathers." All the Utah Ute Indian leaders, with the
exception of Sanpitch, signed this Spanish Fork Treaty.

The Utes assumed they had made a bargain. The U.S. Senate

Survey parties who were "running lines" in Ute country were always at risk of attack. Gunnison was killed with his survey party in 1853. During Powell's 1869 visit with the White River Utes in Colorado, he set stakes during his map-making surveys. He was warned by his guide that the Utes were upset and wanted the stakes removed. In 1875, Dr. Ferdinand Vandeveer Hayden's War Department Survey Party was deep into Ute country on the summit of King Solomon Mountain near Silverton, Colorado, in this photograph. The party was threatened several times but never attacked. W.H. Jackson photo, Hayden, U.S. Geological Survey.

refused to ratify the agreement due to their disagreements with Mormon policies that had nothing to do with the Indians. When the government promises were not met, the Utes returned to raiding and fighting. This period was known as the Black Hawk War. In three years, fifty Mormons and more than three hundred Indians died in the conflicts. Many more Indians, especially young children and older people, died of starvation.

The people of Utah demanded the Utes be removed to a reservation. Brigham Young had sent an expedition to examine the Uintah Valley and determine if it was suitable for Mormon settlements. The expedition reported the area's lack of suitability—even wondering why God had created the area unless it was to hold the other parts of the world together. A month after this expedition returned, Abraham Lincoln set aside this same valley as a reservation for the Utah Utes.

Following the Black Hawk War, the Utah Utes' new leader Tabby-To-Kawana led the remaining Indians to this reservation. From 1869 on they would remain, except for occasional hunting trips that more often than not resulted in complaints about the Indians from settlers.

Gold Fever

In 1858, one word, "GOLD," brought tens of thousands of prospectors and settlers pouring into the Colorado mountains. So many came in such a short time that by February 28, 1861, the Colorado Territory was established to maintain order. A war veteran from the war with Mexico, William Gilpin, was appointed governor and superintendent of Indian Affairs for the new territory.

At this time, all Indians in Colorado were allowed to wander from the agencies where they were assigned to other areas to hunt, gather supplies, or for whatever other purpose they desired. The Utes had ceased raiding and were trying to abide by treaty agreements made previously. Still, there was a great deal of anxiety about what should be done with these wandering Utes.

Colorado Territory Delegate Hiram P. Bennet wrote of his concern to Commissioner of Indian Affairs William Dole in Washington:

> The Indians are variously estimated to number from twelve to twenty thousand. With one half of these Indians at least there is no treaty and hence they are without agents. They are a numerous, brave, and warlike tribe but as yet entirely friendly with the whites of the Territory. They occupy all that part of Colorado Territory west of the Snowy Range of the Rocky Mountains comprising about one half of said Territory. I am justified in saying that a much larger number of miners and prospectors and explorers will go into this country this summer, searching for gold and other precious metals overwhelming the entire country now occupied by these bands of the Utes.
>
> I need not attempt to draw a picture of the horrors of a war of extermination with these numerous and hardy Indians of the Rocky Mountains, nor need I suggest the economy of choosing to treaty with them and feeding them in preference to fighting them at the present time.
>
> For these various considerations I am induced to ask and most seriously urge upon your department the propriety of treating

Magazines and newspapers used sensationalism when dealing with the popular subject of Indians to such an extent that reports and engravings like this one were often misleading. These "wild and disheveled" people were sketched during imprisonment at Fort Utah near Provo following an 1850 Mormon retaliation for raids. They hardly resemble homeless, frightened Ute women and children. The American Heritage Book of Indians, Utah State Historical Society.

Well-mounted and heavily armed Utes came to Salt Lake City occasionally to sell horses, or to receive distribution of rations that were often traded for whiskey or other items of little value before they left town. This photo labeled "On the road to a grand Pow-Wow" was taken c. 1870 in front of the Eagle Emporium, now the State Bank of Utah on the corner of 1st Street and Main. Utah State Historical Society.

Denver residents were used to the familiar sight of Utes wandering the streets after the Denver Agency was established there in 1871 to distribute rations to the roving Utes headed for the plains to hunt buffalo. This group, escorted by agent Willard Patten, was invited to Denver in September 1882 to do a war dance at the National Mining Exposition Celebration. W.H. Jackson photo, Colorado Historical Society.

with the Ute Indians of Colorado Territory in such manner as to extinguish their title to the mineral land of Colorado and to preserve the public peace therein.

Only a few weeks after Gilpin was assigned as governor of Colorado Territory he sent a report on the state of Colorado Territory in relation to Indians, agencies, minerals, and excellence of the territory. (Condensed.)

June 19th, 1861

To: the Hon. William P. Dole,
Commissioner of Indian Affairs
Washington City

Since my arrival here (May 27th) I have been necessarily occupied in perfecting my knowledge of this territory and its people and Indians. This scrutiny has acquainted me with the most wonderful array of facts. The fertility of the soil, the metals, the climate, the scenery, are all of a superlative excellence. These all surpass my most extravagant expectations. Denver City has a location at once adjacent to the mountain system and to the Great Plains. Accessible to all the great roads upon the line of travel and commerce between the two oceans.

The population as you will see by the imperfect census inclosed, exceeds 30,000 nearly all able bodied men. This is the equivalent of 130,000 where society is complete in its details. This combination of labor stimulated by the tonic atmosphere, health, and gold has produced in two years the most marvelous results. Property in mills, towns, farms, and cattle has accumulated to the amount of many millions. This is scattered and located everywhere, in the gorges of the mountains, upon the great roads, along the river bottoms and on both flanks of the Snowy Cordillera.

Availing myself of a well-selected surveying party conducted by E.L. Berthoud, a skillful Civil Engineer, accompanied by the experienced guide James Bridger, I have instructed agent Vaile to accompany them to visit Salt Lake City and confer with the agency there to ascertain the numbers, and localities of the Indians living within this Superintendency and fit himself to organize his department and locate at Breckenridge beyond the Snowy Cordillera. This region, heretofore little known, turns out to be very attractive and fertile in gold and such lands, swarms of white men are daily washing over the Cordillera and establishing themselves in isolated settlements. The number of Indians is large and the duties of the Agent will soon become arduous and incessant. As soon as Agent Vaile returns from his present tour of discovery and information I will submit a report of what is necessary to be done to insure the threatened tranquility of that quarter of the Territory.

The numerous bands of Indians roam over this whole area and come in contact with the women, the children, the stock and property of all descriptions. Innumerable temptations and opportunities for isolated attack, for theft and debauchery everywhere occur.

To establish and maintain order over so large an area and such a variety of elements is a delicate task. The management of the Indians relations is of first and cardinal interest. These Indians forming twelve distinct bands, all subdivided into wandering villages, having horses, and unrestrained by treaties to any locality; dependent on the chase for existence and hemmed in by roads and lines of settlements, are menaced by fears, which are the immediate prelude of despair and desperation.

The Indians belonging to this Superintendency and who may be said to revolve around this city, as round a center are the:

1. Comanches
   Kiowas   of the Arkansas, Smokey
   Cheyennes   Hill and Republican River
   Arapahos   one Agency (Boone, incumbent)

2. Ogallallah Sioux   South Platte and
   Half Breeds of Arapahos   Cache La Poudre Rivers
   Cheyenne – Sioux   one sub agency

3. Apaches   of the Raton mountains
   Utahs (Tabuaches)   and Rio del Norte
                               (Kit Carson, incumbent)

4. Utah (Mehuaches)   of the Parc of San Louis
   Capote and Navajos   Eagle River and
   Lafayette Head (incumbent) San Juan Mountains

5. Utah of Grand and Green   of the South and Middle and
   rivers and Shoshones or   North parcs and country north
   Snake Indians   and west of parcs. One agency
                               (Harvey M. Vaile, incumbent)

I estimate the aggregate number of these Indians to be 25,000 all of the class of "buffalo Indians" that is, perpetually migrating and subsisting exclusively upon the aboriginal game and stock.

A very complete experience among the "buffalo Indians" spanning over twenty years, enables me to state that the U.S. law regulating intercourse with the Indian tribes is inapplicable to the Great Plains and Mountains. Its enforcement, rigorously, leads point blank to expensive and bloody wars, to the destruction of property, to the massacre of the innocent and the escape of the guilty. The desirable end is to be obtained by the efficient organization of this Superintendency, dealing from the center directly with those surrounding tribes, through the Agents acting in person and promptly, always present to anticipate and decide difficulties and enforce uniform and simple rules of discipline.

Agent A.G. Boone has received and stored at Fort Wise goods forwarded for the Cheyennes and Arapaho for the current season which I have directed him to retain until the Autumn and deliver them at the setting in of cold weather, when the Indians become destitute and importunate. These bands of Indians constantly frequent the settled, central region of Colorado where they claim to have a right to remain permanently. They kill cattle, steal horses and beg and threaten the people. It is most essential to the peace of the region that the confirmation of the existing treaty with these Indians be hastened in order that they may be restrained to their reserve and withdraw from contact with the white population.

The Comanche and Kiowa Indians are in a delicate position. The preparations for a treaty with them were initiated and presents sent out for that purpose. Subsequent war was declared against them by your predecessor, the presents withheld, and the tribes turned loose. They are greatly humbled and perpetually beg for peace. Allow me to advise a treaty with them as soon as possible.

Attention to economy dictates a systematic organization of this Superintendency, efficient to secure the present and prospective police of the Indian and the tranquility of his relation with the white man. The existing loose character of Indian relations here combined with the absence of a military force and confusion incidental to a divided authority responsibility when the military is present, strongly commend it.

I ask therefore for the five Indian agents as above, transportation for Superintendent and Agents to be held and accounted for by them. Interpreters (permanent and occasional), an annual appropriation of $50,000 for the miscellaneous expenses of treaties, annuities, casual maintenance and feeding of Indians and etc. Specific Treaties, to fix the condition and duties of the Indians and define accurately the rules and expenses of the Agents.

Remember, that I arrive here to assume the adjustment of much accumulated disorder without the essential funds, agents, transportation, or authority to enforce order. Have the kindness to act favorably upon my suggestions and carry out the policy which you expressed to me in our conversation at Washington City.

The splendid character of this Territory and its flattering future assures me that my representations will receive from you a prompt and liberal response.

> Very Respectfully, William Gilpin
> Governor, Superintendent of Indian Affairs
> Denver, Colorado Territory

On New Year's Eve of 1861, Harvey M. Vaile, special Indian agent stationed at Breckenridge, wrote about his concern for the Indians in his charge and the large number of miners moving into Indian country:

The Indians would never interfere with the whites if they would not tamper with them, but it is a notorious fact that whenever the white race come in contact with the Indians, they steal or cheat them, give them liquor, and otherwise wrong them until they inspire them with a rebellious spirit and it is impossible for their Agents to prevent their state of affairs entirely hence the necessity of keeping the Indians away from them as much as possible. Although the Indians under my charge are peaceable and quiet they are nevertheless poor—therefore I hope Congress may deem it expedient to make them a small appropriation. I ask only the small sum of six or eight thousand dollars, although this is but a mite for the number of the Indians in my Agency. I think I can keep them quiet with this amount, therefore I will not ask for a greater sum.

Vaile was not in favor of furnishing the Indians with "trinkets and ornaments that neither satisfied their hunger or kept them warm." He preferred to furnish them with staples. His list of requests included: "$2000 to be expended in blankets, $1000 in hickory shirts, $1000 in sugar and coffee, $400 in hardware, knives, files, pans, etc., $200 in hard bread, $100 in flour, $200 in percussion caps, powder, lead, matches, etc."

Vaile felt the discoveries and promise of a rich reward would create great risks on the part of the miners:

> In view of this fact and the utter impossibility of keeping the Indians from committing some depredations upon the whites when they frequently come in contact, I would recommend the propriety of making a treaty with them as early in the Spring as practicable and let them remove from the presence of their white brethren, to a region a little farther west.

Land Deals

The contrast between the Indians' idea of control without ownership of the land, and members of the new culture, who felt empty land was going to waste and was therefore available for individual gain and ownership, would cause a tragic clash. The Indian way of life would be lost forever as an entrepreneurial culture determined to develop the West proceeded to remove and/or change anyone or anything that impeded its progress. For their own safety and ease of control, the newcomers needed to remove the Indians to controlled areas. There an attempt could be made to impose the newcomers' economic values and religion on the Indians while overlooking any merits the indigenous culture might have and forbidding them to practice their own culture or religion. The die was cast.

There was gold and silver everywhere in Ute country, and nothing—not orders from the government to stay off of Ute lands nor fear of death—kept the prospectors, miners, or surveyors out of Ute country. The clamor for ownership of Ute lands was thunderous. Remarkably, few miners were attacked or killed by the Utes. The Ute people and the government began a new war—a war of words.

There were many outstanding Ute negotiators and leaders during this difficult time but none were as famous as Ouray and his wife, Chipeta. Ouray's intelligence, fair-mindedness, ability to speak several languages, and an awareness of the power of the United States government made Ouray the government's choice to speak on behalf of all the Utes. Ouray's influence over the entire

The 1868 Treaty commissioners. From left to right: D.C. Oakes (White River Agency, Northern Colorado), Kit Carson (Utah Agency, New Mexico), Lafayette Head (Conejos Agency, Colorado), and Hiram P. Bennet (Colorado Territory delegate). These men accompanied representatives from the Tabeguache, Moache, Capote, Weeminuche, Yampa, Grand River, and Uintah bands of Ute Indians to Washington where the treaty was signed. This treaty provided a single reservation for all these Ute bands with agencies at Los Pinos and Grand River, Colorado. The area that was to be theirs forever was almost the entire western slope of Colorado. Unfortunately this was an area rich in minerals and agricultural lands that settlers and miners wanted to possess. Future treaties would take almost all this land from the Utes. Southwest Museum, Los Angeles, California.

Pine River Store and Post Office on the Los Pinos Agency, located twelve miles west of Cochetopa Pass in Colorado, was set up on Los Pinos Creek in 1869. At agency stores, the Utes could trade buckskins, beadwork, and furs for supplies. They received weekly rations at the agency. Alferd Packer stumbled into this agency during the winter of 1873 after cannibalizing a group of prospectors he was guiding. (1) is Agent Charles Adams, and (3) may be George Bent. Center of Southwest Studies, Fort Lewis College.

Ute nation was held by his own strength of character, swift retaliation against those who doubted his word or acted without his consent, and a power of reasoning that everyone could understand and admire.

Ouray summarized the Ute situation at a meeting with Kit Carson, Governor A. Cameron Hunt, and others when they were trying to persuade the Indians to move onto a reservation to restore their health and wealth. "True! so; a heap! (Now) Utes got plenty. But soon all gone, and then Utes starve a heap. Long time ago, Utes always had plenty. On the prairie, antelope and buffalo, so many Ouray can't count. In the mountains, deer and bear everywhere. In the streams, trout, duck, beaver, everything. Good Manitou gave all to red man: Utes happy all the year. White men came, now Utes go hungry a heap. Game much go every year hard to shoot now. Old man often weak for want of food. Squaw and papoose cry. Only strong brave live, white man grow a heap; red man no grow—Soon die all."

Kit Carson Treaty

On March 2, 1868, a treaty known as the Kit Carson Treaty was signed. It provided that all of the Colorado Utes would be placed on about 1,500,000 acres of land in western Colorado, known as the Confederated Ute Reservation, for their "absolute and undisturbed use and occupation." The rest of their lands were to be ceded— opened for settlement.

The Utes were reluctant to sign this treaty, but they did sign. Chief Ouray was quoted as saying that the Utes signed the treaty only with the understanding that the "Government should strike out all that relates to mill, machinery, farming, schools, and going onto a reservation." The Utes were opposed to settling down in one place. Tradition taught them that remaining in one place meant death.

Feelings of concern, hopelessness, and bitterness ran like strong currents between the Indians, settlers, and the government officials. "They had a national pride and patriotism," Powell noted of the Utes. "His peace with other tribes, his home and livelihood for his family are his interests, everything that is dear to him is associated with his country." Many white men had little understanding of these Indian values. The Utes could hardly be expected to feel friendly toward the men fencing and farming land that had been theirs.

Special Agent Harvey Vaile reported: "Something must be done for the Indians or necessity would compel them to rob and steal in order to stay alive."

Quotes from this era reveal clearly the conflicts taking place:

"The Indian Department does not feed them . . . We have taken their land, driven their game away, and now to kill them for committing depredations solely to save life cannot be justified."

General James Carlton

"We do not want to sell a foot of our land—that is the opinion of all . . . The whites can go and take the gold and come out again. We do not want them to build houses there."

Ouray

"The buffalo that once swarmed in these mountain parks, the ancient home of these people, have all disappeared since the settlement of the country by the white men; hence the almost starving condition we find them in today."

English traveler William Blackmore

"They will have to freeze and starve a little more, I reckon, before they will listen to common sense."

General William Sherman

"The whole business is a monotonous piece of treachery and bloodstained villainy in which innocent persons suffer, while scoundrels who cheat and swindle the poor Indians keep out of danger and fill their pockets with money."

Josephine Meeker

"Such an agreement as the buffalo makes with his hunters when pierced with arrows; all he can do is to lie down and cease every attempt to escape or resist."

Ute Council

"There is no use of making a long ado about the Indian question, the only solution of the problem is extermination."

Boulder, Colorado Banner, October 1878

Gradually all the Utes in Colorado and Utah were assigned to an agency where blankets, food, and other supplies were supposed to be distributed on a regular basis. The Utes were encouraged to remain in the area near their assigned agency. However, there was no government policy to force the Utes stay in one area. If they wanted to collect their rations they had to appear in person at their assigned agency, and if they didn't want the rations they simply didn't show up for them.

Private Peter Tawse, stationed with troops on the Uncompahgre River, wrote this description of ration day in his diary on May 17, 1880.

There were no Indians around the agency, they live over in the mountain parks and come into the agency every Saturday to draw their rations. It was great to see about five hundred Indian bucks and squaws all mounted on ponies. [It is] when they came to collect the beef that the sport commences. The beef are all put in a corral, one beef is given to so many Indians, when they commence to kill the cattle one Indian who is known to be a good shot, he it is that does the most of the shooting but before they are all killed the rest of the Indians commence and shoot from all directions and it becomes very dangerous. The Indians will not eat the liver. The squaws do the most of the cutting up of the beef. They cut and slash it up in all kinds of pieces. Everything is used up but the horns. After cattle are killed the Indians all go into horse racing, where there is quite a number of dollars and blanket and moneys exchange hands. They are very earnest in their races.

The Utes continued to wander from their agency areas, trying to supplement their meager or missing rations by hunting and gathering as they always had. They would show up hundreds of miles from the agency assigned to them and attempt to draw rations from whatever agency they were near. Most of the time they were issued rations only at the agency they were assigned to. The Denver Agency was established in 1871 as a base for supplies where the wandering Utes could draw supplies for their annual buffalo hunts. Officials had decided it was less expensive to let Utes go off the reservation to hunt than to train them to be farmers on their reservation.

According to Major James Thompson, special agent for the Utes in Colorado Territory:

The government issued annuities to practically all of its Indian wards, and the issuance to the Utes was made by me in Denver. They would come here to meet me in great number. I have had as high as a thousand of them here at one time. Their favorite camping place was in the Platte bottoms just across the river from the mouth of Cherry Creek. Here they would set up their tepees and sometimes remain for several weeks, coming into town almost every day and walking around and gazing into the store windows for amusement.

The Platte bottoms where Denver is located was a favorite place for great encampments like this one in 1874. A man's war shield is hung on the tripod outside his tepee. Clothing and bedding is aired out on these same tripods. Smithsonian Institution.

There were many reported encounters with the "friendly Utes" from miners, settlers, and travelers. The Utes seemed to make a game of frightening the intruders but seldom caused serious problems; more often they tried to barter for supplies. Hester McClung wrote in her diary of an encounter with a village of fifty tepees near where they were camped in 1873:

> When we saw them in Denver I thought nothing could induce me to touch them, but here upon closer acquaintance we considered some of them kind and agreeable friends, and our antipathy for them vanished to such an extent that three of them ate at the table with us the last morning. These three were their greatest men—the civil chief, Yah-man, their war chief, Washington, and Bill . . . they were enough civilized to wear hats, though they still adhere to their paint, beads, blankets, and leggings . . . the constant demand made on our larder by their frequent enquiry for biscuit, that one word standing for all articles of food, forced us to turn back toward civilization to replenish our stock of provisions.

Near Tabernash, Colorado, the Utes turned their horses into a rancher's fenced pasture, a disagreement followed, and Chief Tabernash was shot. The next rancher the Utes met while retreating, even though he was a known friend, was killed in retaliation. Indian reasoning was, "Indian good—he no know he be killed. White man shoot um. White man good man, he no know he be killed, Indian shoot um, all same." It was the old code of the West, "an eye for an eye" with one exception. If a white man killed an Indian it was a justified, heroic deed in most cases; if an Indian killed it was murder or a massacre.

Brunot Treaty

Trouble continued to develop between the wandering Indians and the wave of settlers and miners swarming into the mountains, resulting in the U.S. government sending Felix Brunot, president of the U.S. Board of Indian Commissioners, to negotiate a new treaty. The Brunot Agreement was the most devastating and confining treaty the Ute people ever signed. Brunot made many promises, including finding Ouray's son who had been captured by the Arapaho while the Indians were on a buffalo hunt many years earlier.

Ouray was given a yearly salary of $1,000 to act as spokesman for the Ute people and agent for the United States. Brunot advised the Indians to make and keep a treaty. They were told that this would be the last request the government would ever make of the

Colorado Utes in Washington, D.C. in 1874 following a three-month trip through the East that cost over fifteen thousand dollars. The trip and a meeting with President Grant was to impress the Indians with the wisdom of signing the Brunot Agreement, which gave miners access to the San Juan Mountains in Colorado. Front row, left to right: Guero, Chipeta, Ouray, Piah (Ouray's brother). Middle row: Uriah M. Curtis, Interpreter; James B. Thompson, Denver Ute agent; Charles Adams, Los Pinos agent; Otto Mears, government negotiator and interpreter. Back row: Washington, possibly Susan (Ouray's sister), Johnston No. 2, Captain Jack, John. Colorado Historical Society.

Utes. Brunot encouraged them saying, "Some men say, let this matter go on, let it alone and it will fix itself, there will be trouble with the Utes and then we will get their country for nothing."

A group of Ute leaders were taken to Washington to confer with the White Father about this new treaty. They were dazzled with parties, carriages, new suits, and other pleasures available in the capital city. In 1873, after repeated protests, the Utes signed the agreement forfeiting rights to the majority of the land they had been given in the former treaties.

The Meeker Tragedy

As predicted, trouble with the Utes did result with the Utes being confined to reservations. The year 1879 was disastrous for the Utes and their agent Nathan C. Meeker. Meeker, the agent assigned to the White River Agency in Northern Colorado early in 1878, was persistent in his belief that a stern example would civilize the White River Utes. He pushed them to build houses and fences and to farm. He pushed the wrong Utes. These men considered themselves horsemen, members of the warrior society of Utes, but never farmers. They went along with him at times, but when he insisted on plowing the meadow that they used as a racetrack, they warned him in no uncertain terms that he had gone too far. Chief Johnson had an argument with Meeker and pushed him down. Other Utes fired warning shots at the farm help when they started the plowing. Meeker sent for the army to help him enforce his will.

Many of these Utes had been scouts for the army. They knew what usually happened when the army was called against Indians. They considered Meeker's calling the army a declaration of war. Ute scouts met the approaching army and warned it not to come onto the reservation lands, which was prohibited by treaty agreement with Governor Pitkin. The soldiers continued their march and were attacked. The commander, Major Thomas Thornburgh, was killed and his entire force surrounded and held where they were for several days until Captain Francis S. Dodge and his cavalry of black "Buffalo Soldiers" rode to their rescue.

At the agency, Meeker and all other male employees were killed. The three women and two children living at the agency were taken into the mountains and held captive for twenty-three days.

This was the leverage needed by the Colorado citizens to force the Utes remaining in Colorado onto reservations. Colorado Governor F.W. Pitkin made the following statement to the press.

It will be impossible for the Indians and whites to live in peace hereafter . . . This attack had no provocation and the whites now understand that they are liable to be attacked in any part of the state . . . My idea is that, unless removed by the government they must necessarily be exterminated.

The Colorado Utes stood together in protecting the Indians who had participated in the Meeker killings and the fight with Thornburgh's troops. On January 16, 1880, a troop of soldiers and Otto Mears, who was to serve as interpreter, accompanied a small group of Utes, including Ouray and his wife Chipeta, to Washington, D.C., to negotiate their fate with officials of the Bureau of Indian Affairs.

"Unwelcome Citizens" read the Washington *Post* headline on January 22, 1880. Secretary Schurz sent for a portion of the Utes to

JACK   THORNBURGH   DOUGLAS   ANTELOPE

The Meeker Tragedy was the last major Indian uprising in the United States. On October 25, 1879, Harpers Weekly ran a story on the Ute War with these etchings.

Captain Jack had made a trip to the agency in Denver to complain that Meeker was causing trouble and was unfit as agent. He and Johnson had served as scouts for the army. They had seen troops sent against Indians before and realized the Indians would come out losers. He was very upset and warned the troops that it would be a mistake to bring the soldiers to the reservation.

Major Thomas T. Thornburgh was in command of the troops sent to aid Agent Meeker at the White River Agency. He agreed to halt his troops outside the reservation, but for some unknown reason pushed on and was ambushed at Milk Creek, where he was killed in the first outburst of firing. The troops were held trapped for two days.

Old Chief Douglas was held responsible for the attack on the soldiers and the killing of Meeker and his employees at the agency. While in the company of other Ute men on their way to Washington to talk over their problems in 1880, he was removed from the train and held without charge at Fort Leavenworth. He was the only Indian personally punished although the White River Utes had monies paid to survivors and widows of the Meeker Tragedy from their annuities for twenty years.

Antelope, Chief Ouray's runner, was sent to the White River Utes with a message from Ouray advising them to release the captives. Former agent and friend of the Utes Charles Adams traveled to the White River Camp, where he succeeded in bargaining for the captives' release. Virginia Shippey collection.

host another consultation. The subject discussed was the removal of the Utes from their present locations. Senator Hill and Mr. Belford made the demand that "these Indians be removed altogether from Colorado. Senator Teller is willing to have them removed to reservations in the eastern part of the state, and is supported in this by Ouray."

"The Utes Must Go" was the headline in the same paper just five days later. Colorado Governor Pitkin had just arrived in Washington. He told reporters, "The people of Colorado regard them (Utes) as a menace; a source of danger; an impediment to the opening of the best lands in the state. Every year several counties are warned

Ouray, chief of the Utes, and his wife, Chipeta, pose for their last formal photograph together in Washington, D.C., in January 1880. By August, Ouray was dead. He was saved the sorrow of seeing his wife and his people herded to Utah to live on reservations. Ouray shunned the business suits provided for Washington visitors. He preferred to wear and be photographed in his native attire. Chipeta was the belle of Washington, her dress described as white as cotton and nearly as soft as silk. Smithsonian Institution.

by these Indians that if they do not leave they will be killed. The Indians do not abide on their reservations, but are constantly roaming off from it, plundering and devastating. The people of Colorado are exposed to the unchecked violence of worthless savages, whose pastime is destroying life and property, ravishing women, and other similar exploits of irredeemable barbarians." When asked what remedy he would suggest, he replied, "The Utes must go."

After days and days of testimony before congressional committees, the "Washington Treaty" was signed with an X by Shavano, Alhandra, Veratzityz, Galota, Jocknick, Wass, Sowawick, and Ignacio. Ouray was the only Indian to sign his own name to the document. The Utes who had occupied southern Colorado, New Mexico, and Arizona were already living on a reservation assigned to them at Ignacio, Colorado, in 1877. They were allowed to remain where they were. The lands formerly held in common by a tribe, however, were to be assigned in certain proportions to each individual Indian. The rest of their lands would be sold in exchange for allotments of land in severalty with certain annuities. The rest of the Utes in Colorado, guilty for what happened to Meeker or not, were to be moved to reservations in Utah.

A Ute commission was set up to carry out the provisions of the treaty. The commissioners—J.J. Russell, Otto Mears, and Thomas McMorris—recommended:

> Until the Indians can be made somewhat familiar with their new relations, it is . . . of vital importance to maintain the exterior boundary limits of the lands upon which they dwell as a reservation, and within which white men may not be allowed to locate. This protection may be secured by legislation or possibly be executive order. For years to come these Indians should certainly have the aid of the government in protecting them from collision with white men.

It was necessary that three-fourths of the Ute males sign this agreement for it to be legal. Otto Mears, interpreter, pioneer road builder, and the commissioner appointed to secure the signatures, described his part in getting this accomplished: "We made a treaty with the Indians for the Western Slope . . . The government was paying two dollars an acre for every acre . . . the Indians would not believe the government, so I gave them two dollars each (those who signed the treaty) and they said the two dollars was worth more than all the government promised."

Ouray would not have to witness his people's banishment from Colorado. Before all the signatures could be obtained, Ouray died

*Ute leaders representing all of the Ute people were taken to Washington to nego-
tiate their fate following the Meeker incident. Negotiations for a new treaty that
favored the Ute point of view were dependent on the surrender of the Ute men responsible for the Meeker killings. When this condition could not or would not be
met by the Utes, the Washington officials concluded the negotiations in their favor.
The Ute men in these photographs would be the last to have lived traditional lives
on their native lands. Now they would have to sign a paper that would remove the
people they were responsible for to reservations where they would live forever as
virtual prisoners.* Jan Pettit collection. Ute Pass Historical Society.

Galota (1), Otto Mears (2), Severo (3), Shavano (4), Col. H. Page (5), Jocknick (6).

*Ignacio (7), Carl Schurz, Secretary of the Interior (8), Woretsiz (9), Ouray (10),
Gen. Charles Adams (11), Chipeta (12).*

Ojo Blanco (13), William H. Berry (14), Tap-uch (15), Captain Jack (16), Tim Johnson (17).

Sowawick (18), Henery Jim (19), Buckskin Charlie (20), Wass (21), William Burns (22), Alhandra (23).

from what the doctors thought was kidney trouble. He had refused the medical doctor's treatment, preferring the traditional medicine man's treatment. Within an hour of his death near the agency building in Ignacio on the Southern Ute Reservation, the entire group of Indian tepees were struck and moved over a mile away as was the custom of the Utes. Ouray's body was wrapped in blankets, tied on the back of his favorite horse, and led away to a traditional Ute burial in a crevice covered with rocks somewhere in the mountains.

The day after his death, newspaper headlines read, "The death of Ouray on the 24th of August, 1880 was a blow from which the Ute nation will never recover. The greatest Indian that ever lived is dead and there is no one to fill his place."

In 1925 the remains of Ouray's body were supposedly exhumed and buried with great ceremony at the agency cemetery. The elders of the tribe maintain the belief that the location of Ouray's body was never revealed. Ouray most likely still lies in his final resting place.

With sad hearts, the Uncompahgre and White River Utes were escorted toward their new homes in the valleys of the White and Green rivers by four companies of cavalry under the command of General R. MacKenzie. In September 1881, they crossed the Grand (Colorado) and Green rivers on large boats built for their use. For many years after, western emigrants used the boats to ferry across the same rivers. Broken in spirit and body, the Utes left the lush, green mountain homelands of their ancestors, forbidden to return. Colorado Historical Society.

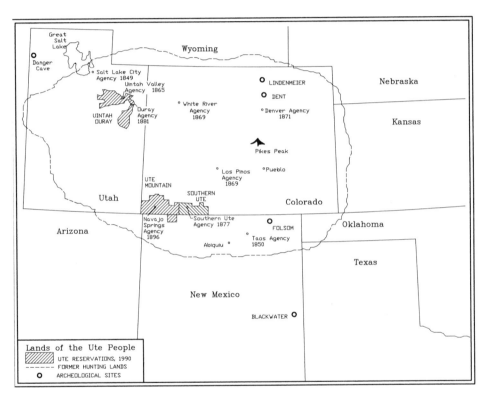

Ute reservations and archaeological sites, 1990. The Ute people hold the largest reservation in Utah and are the only Indians holding reservations in Colorado. Wars, starvation, and disease depleted the Ute population from approximately 8,000 in 1859 to half that many twenty years later. Population decline continued until the 1920s; by then it had decreased by half again, leaving only about 2,000 Ute people. From that time on Ute population has increased; the 1970 census report showed a population of close to 4,000 Utes. Sixty-five percent of this number lived on one of the three Ute reservations.

This group of Utes camped in Cheyenne Canyon near Colorado Springs. Seated in the center front row is Chipeta. Requests for groups of Ute people to attend celebrations came from all over Colorado after the Utes were confined to reservations. The Ute dances and beautiful outfits were a popular attraction. Photo c. 1913, Virginia Stumbough collection, Ute Pass Historical Society.

Chapter 6
The Reservation Years

If the old saying "Out of sight out of mind" was supposed to solve the Ute problem, it didn't.

The Uintah Utes were already having a hard time supporting themselves by hunting and farming on the arid lands of their Uintah Valley Reservation. They objected to more Indians being placed on their lands. Objections and refusal to move to the reservations were to no avail. All the Utes were now removed to reservations in Colorado and Utah. They were not supposed to leave the boundaries of their assigned area.

When the last Ute Indians were assigned to a reservation, Secretary of the Interior Carl Schurz was in charge of all United States Indian affairs. He had formulated an Indian policy that called for the "civilization" of the natives of America. He opposed their removal to reservations, feeling they should accept allotments of land where they were currently living and live like their neighbors. This meant they should be taught English, learn to read and write, become agriculturally oriented, wear white men's clothing, and live in houses. In other words they should become "carbon-copy white men." His policy was the guideline followed by those who followed him. Schurz felt he had the Indians' welfare in mind when he made his recommendations. Ouray considered him one of the few friends the Utes had in Washington.

By the turn of the century each reservation had been assigned a superintendent whose duties included distributing goods and developing programs for the Utes' progress toward being civilized. Allotments and annuities varied from group to group depending on treaty agreements, provisions, land allocation, leases, sales, and so on.

Although the Utes had been promised reservations for their "absolute and undisturbed use and occupation," the Uintah-Ouray and

Southern Ute reservations have been checkerboarded with non-Indian land owners as a result of the passage of the Dawes Severalty Act, which provided individual allotment of tracts to each Indian. The remainder of the land promised to the Utes as a reservation was eventually opened for settlement. Forest preserves, state and national parks, mining claims, highways, and railways have further divided their lands.

In recent years the tribes have purchased some of these allotments from Indian and non-Indian owners and returned them to tribal ownership. The Ute Indian people have never been comfortable with the allotment system. Their centuries-old culture teaches a communal system that does not fit well with individual pursuit of gain and individual ownership of land.

The Next Fifty Years

Covering the development, progress, and problems at each reservation would take several volumes. Instead, included here is a sampling of stories, reports from government officials and agents, and portions of letters from various Utes, traders, and their neighbors with the hope that this overview will provide a sense of what has happened between the time the Utes were placed on reservations and the present.

After being confined to reservations, the fearless, active men who had formerly spent their time hunting, fishing, clearing the campsite, gathering tepee poles, butchering meat, making rope, building fires, and supplying tools and other necessities for their families were obliged to become sedentary. The warrior exchanged his healthful tepee for an overheated cabin, and his diet of fresh meat, berries, and seeds, loaded with vitamins and minerals, was replaced by flour and salted meat. There were noticeable changes in the Utes' physical condition. Many Utes no longer had ambition or energy, but instead brooded on the past and became bitter.

"I had been a brave man," said Chief Buckskin Charlie. "I had fought the enemies of my tribe by day and by night; I had something to think about all the time, and got the full enjoyment out of the busy and active days as they passed. But now I had nothing to do but eat and sleep and be lazy like a child. The dullness of my life took away all the pleasure of living. I will not be sorry when my time comes to die." He believed that the only alternative left for his people was to strive to learn to read and write and farm, and do the other things that are done by the white people, but he had grave doubts as to whether his people would ever be able to succeed in the new life that was being forced upon them.

Depending on rations for their families was hard on these people used to wandering the hills and valleys gathering food and hunting for their livelihood. Many times the rations were barely adequate to ward off starvation and the rations were not the type of mineral- and vitamin-rich food they were used to eating.

Indian men were responsible for providing meat for their families and felt a strong need to hunt. In 1887, Colorow led a small band on a hunting expedition into Colorado. They were attacked by the game warden and his posse of ranchers and accused of illegally poaching game. Before the Indians could retaliate, the militia was called out to return the wanderers to their reservation.

White River Utes Starr and Snake Pete and about thirty other Indians moved into the Lily Park area of Colorado to hunt. Game wardens again raided their camp, where they found forty or fifty green deer hides, and tried to arrest the Indians. The Indians refused to go, a scramble resulted, and when all was over one Ute woman was shot and two Indian men lay dead.

The year 1914 rolled around and the Utes were still leaving the reservation to go hunting in Colorado and Wyoming just as they always had. Now they got in trouble for not having a license. When they heard the price of a license many decided not to go hunting; "deer hunting cost too much," some said. Shavanaux and twelve other Indians ignored the rules and slipped away to hunt on Douglas Creek in Colorado. The Game and Fish commissioner of Colorado was sent a message as soon as the Utes were reported missing from their reservation. Before it was over Colorado was in alarm, and rumors about the hunting party placed its size at up to eight hundred hunters who were slaughtering deer, instead of the original twelve. By the time the Indian police caught up with the hunters, they had one deer among them and were heading back to the reservation. The report to Washington stated that "The Indians of this reservation are not very far advanced in the sciences of civilization. They still possess to a strong degree the habits and desires of their ancestors; and will continue for some years to come to cause these little difficulties, but they will grow less and less as time goes by."

Getting supplies to the Utah agencies was often a problem. Freighters brought supplies to the new Ouray, Utah agency through the canyon from Price via the Denver and Rio Grande Railroad or through Dragon from the Uintah Railroad Supply Station. Delivery of the staple goods depended on weather, available freighters, railroad service, agent funds, and other problems, which often delayed delivery of the goods the Ute people depended upon from several weeks to several months. Surrounding neighbors complained regularly to Washington about having to feed the starving Indians.

Escape to South Dakota

By 1905 each Uintah and White River Ute was to be allotted 80 acres of land on the reservation. The remaining land was to be sold and "proceeds used for the benefit of the Indians." The Utes objected. Those who refused to choose allotments were assigned allotments that were not always the best land available.

The White River Utes requested removal from the reservation as the whites rushed in to claim the land for settlement and farms. Denial of their request provoked a mass exodus in 1906 of more than 300 White River and Uncompahgre Utes accompanied by a few leaders of the Uintah band. Under the leadership of Red Cap,

Delegation from Uintah-Ouray Reservations traveled to Washington in 1905 to plead with the government not to sell their reservation lands. To no avail—lands were allotted to each Indian and the remaining land was opened for settlement. Front row, left to right: Appah, Arrive. Center: Red Cap, David Copperfield, Charlie Shavanaux, Wee-che. Back row: Wallace Stark, Charley Mack, John Duncan, Suckive, Unknown, Boco White, Unknown. Utah Historical Society.

White River Chief Red Cap and his family. Several hundred Utes followed Red Cap to South Dakota in 1906 to protest their lands being opened to white settlement. They were held as prisoners of war on the Sioux reservation for two years until they decided to return to their Utah reservation, discouraged and defeated by lack of supplies and lack of support from their Sioux and Crow neighbors. Photograph taken in January, 1907. C.C. McBride photographer, Smithsonian Institution.

they loaded their belongings on wagons and horses and started for South Dakota, where they hoped to form an alliance with the Sioux and Crow to bring a stop to the land allotment program.

U.S. Army troops converged upon the group and escorted them to Fort Meade, South Dakota where they were detained as prisoners of war. They were temporarily settled on a portion of the Sioux reservation. Their annuities were frozen to cover expenses incurred in caring for them in South Dakota. By spring of 1907 many were in dire need of clothing. A total of $1,042.50 worth of clothing was shipped to the fort from the Bloom Shoe and Clothing Company in Sturgis, South Dakota, and from the Bennett Co. and J.L. Brandies & Sons in Omaha, Nebraska. The men were given 115 blankets, vests, trousers, shirts, hats, and coats. Women received 1150 yards of calico in all colors and 200 yards of camp cloth, shoes, and stockings. The children were issued similar clothing. The cost of all the

"Four Ute Indian Agitators." Red Cap's young warriors pose in ceremonial dress for a photograph taken during their confinement near Sturgis, South Dakota. Left to right: (1) Chuponas (Dave Weech) is wearing a bear claw necklace and holding a bone whistle; (2) Pompy; (3) Apona also wears a bear claw necklace and sports a gun, as does (4) Rainbow, mounted on his horse holding a rifle he was photographed with at other times. This is the only rifle in any of the South Dakota photographs. Apparently their weapons were not taken from them. Lying on the trade blanket in the foreground are a bow and arrows. Hanging on the shrub is Red Cap's trade blanket decorated with a wide beaded strip usually worn by chiefs. C.C. McBride photographer, Smithsonian Institution.

clothing was deducted from their annuities. Charges to each individual vary from 95 cents for most of the children's supplies to $22.50 charged to Dave Weech Chuponas.

Conditions were no better on the Sioux reservation in South Dakota than they were in Utah. After two years of disappointment the Utes were escorted back to their Utah reservation.

Indian Farmers

Attempts were made time and again to interest the Utes in farming. The Indians were willing to wear the white man's clothes, eat his food, and even pray to his God, but farming was considered degrading and undignified. Ute elder Suckive expressed his disgust for farming when he stated firmly that he "would not live like a pig in a pen."

Farming experts were hired to help the Utes learn to farm. When the program started the government farmers were doing most of the farming themselves. The resistance on the part of the Indians to farming and cultural changes was as strong as the government's determination to change them and would eventually cause the loss of even more land.

By 1922, many of the Utes were farming, although most were not considered to be living in suitable dwellings. The 1922 Indian Service report noted that the "ideal farm-home" concept needed "to be impressed upon the mind of every Native American." The report noted that forty percent of the Indians were "not living on their allotments, do not till the soil, do not own stock, take no interest in public affairs, keep their eyes continually turned backward, keep their minds occupied with old grievances. They must be gotten out of the brush. If left to their own wallow they will die there. Every Indian possesses the nucleus of a desirable home where he could make himself and family happy and contented. If there be anything lacking, it is the desire on the part of the individual." Uintah-Ouray Superintendent F.A. Gross proposed an ambitious five-year industrial program that would change attitudes and instill ambition.

This "Awakening Project" was designed to encourage the Indians to become "self-reliant, self-supporting, self-respecting citizens. That is the one and only purpose in maintaining the Indian Bureau."

Goals included having every Indian build a house, plant a garden with the food they liked (such as melons, corn, potatoes, and squash), a potato tract, and fruit tracts for the children to care for. Men were to plant crops, including alfalfa seed, barley, corn, and fall wheat. Farming, raising poultry and stock, and beekeeping were to be taught to everyone, starting at grade school level.

The innovative plans to achieve these goals were positive, encouraging, and worked well. "A direct campaign with six or eight cars to hurl fifty of them (Indians) around the circle (of successful farms) in a day will do much toward getting them stirred up," wrote the superintendent. The Indians were to be encouraged to develop their own plans and goals at monthly meetings that were followed by a "big feed."

It was at these meetings that the superintendent hoped to create a "hatred of the marriage and divorce custom, the gambling custom, and the peyote eating custom, by moulding and creating public opinion." He hoped to encourage new leaders—those who were successful in the industrial plan. At one of the meetings Red Cap stated that he felt "everyone should feel friendly towards this movement," but for himself he said he was "still an Indian and could not surrender any of his Indian ways and thought." The only talk at this meeting in opposition was made by Soccioff, who recalled that an old Indian chief had advised them never to farm. Most opposition to farming came from the White River band.

District farmers were expected to keep a card file on each family's progress. They were to attend country and state fairs and educational programs and at all times keep in mind the long list of good advice concerning their attitude and approach to helping the Indians. "All eyes must be directed to the present and to the future, the past must be forgotten. Talk must be directed to practical, everyday problems. Talk works wonders, and we must furnish the leaven for these talks. Sow seeds for thought, never stop to argue, let them do the talking, keep the atmosphere full of progressive ideas, request, never command, believe, never doubt. Personal contact is sure to win. Study the problems, they grow and solve themselves before the man who seeks wisdom rather than imparts it."

Each industrial program had a slogan: "Put a machine shed on every farm," "A few ewes in every hog pasture," "Pleasant homes for pleasant people." The intended results were to have a dairy cow on every farm, horse breeding programs, weed control, good crops, irrigation, improved roads, as well as encouraging Indians to assume community responsibility and improving morals that were not up to government standards. The hope was for Indian farmers to be admitted to agricultural colleges and to lead white farmers in good farm practices. This did happen!

Ute chiefs and subchiefs gathered for the reburial of Chief Ouray in 1925. Left to right are Naneese, Joseph Price, Colorow, Buckskin Charlie, McCook, Pevaga, Pegary, Antonio Buck. George L. Beam photo, Colorado Historical Society.

In just three years Superintendent G.A. Gross was reporting encouraging progress and sending pages of photographs as positive proof of progress to the commissioner of Indian Affairs. Gross bragged about Patsey Shavanaux's trip to the state fair in Salt Lake City where he had won first prize for his Junior Boys Club garden products exhibit. The agent noted that Patsey stayed with his projects daily and that the son's interest encouraged the father, Sam Alhandra, to get involved in cutting hay, planting wheat, and alfalfa. These efforts were so successful that "Sam now believes farming pays."

"A great future is before these Indians and they seem to realize it. The fact that their annuities have been discontinued has helped to spur them on in their work. They never worked as much before in their history," wrote Superintendent Gross.

Consolidated Ute Agency

Moache, Capote, and Weeminuche bands had been settled on one reservation, referred to as the Southern Ute Reservation, under a treaty negotiated in 1873. Several agencies were combined as the Consolidated Ute Reservation in 1918.

Indian fairs became a big event on the Southern Ute Reservation starting in 1907. At first the Indians were judged separately but by 1916 the Utes were in open competition with their neighbors. The Indians did well with their exhibits and won their fair share or more of prizes. The Durango newspaper reported "Awards given out yesterday show that the agency and farm has not a single 'loafing Indian.' The Utes have been successful, [as] perhaps no other reservation in the United States could boast in a competition with whites at a county fair." The superintendent reported there were no Indian dances (which were discouraged) at any of the fairs.

General Conditions

In 1916 there were ten births at the Southern Ute Agency and ten deaths. Of these deaths, seven were of infants less than three years of age—a high mortality rate. The physician reported, "They do not use peyote and drinking is on the decline since Colorado became dry."

The 1916 report noted that Southern Ute drinking water was obtained from the clean snow-fed streams. "The water here at this place is the best in the world. There are a few privies among the Indians. They mostly use the open sagebrush for this purpose."

The Indians began building adobe homes to live in. The 1916 Southern Ute Agency report noted:

> Most of the homes are supplied with tables, benches, chairs, and cooking stoves. The great majority have beds while the remaining sleep on the floors; those that sleep on the floor have frequent colds because of drafts. They are not accustomed to [drafts], as the tepees are banked up with straw and other material which will exclude drafts. The homes have fireplaces and at least two windows.

By 1925, Agent McKean reported that there were no families living in tents or tepees of any kind among the Southern Ute—they all had houses of either log, adobe, or frame construction.

Schools

The first attempts to educate Indian children at boarding schools were a failure. Parents refused to send their children away saying, "We are willing to send the children to school, but not away from home, because when they go away they die and we cannot account for it." Many children did die when sent away from home, some became blind or tried to return the long distances to their homes. Eventually, Ute children attended school regularly, even though the schools were run on military lines, by the clock, with uniforms, drills, and regimented duties and punishment—all completely foreign to their culture and teachings at home.

The Teller Institute, a boarding school for Ute children in Grand Junction. Museum of Western Colorado.

The Teller Institute of Grand Junction was opened as a boarding school for Indian students in 1885 through the influence of Senator Henry M. Teller. Ute treaty funds were used to build the school, and the first students were almost grown men, coming from the Uintah reservation in Utah. As time went on, the school was attended by more Navajo, Papago, Moquis, Shoshone, and Pima Indians than Ute. This was also true of boarding schools at the Consolidated Ute Agency. By 1908, the school had grown from one small building to twelve. Five were sturdy brick buildings. At the peak of its enrollment, the school had two hundred Indian children. When the school closed in 1911, the equipment was sold, the funds reverted to the government, and the buildings were allowed to go to ruin.

Games included boys' baseball, girls' basketball, and group games for small children. One school inspector was concerned because there was no stereopticon available for amusement. The school in Utah was much like the one at the Southern Ute Agency. A visiting physician reported, "It has seldom been my pleasure to

Mandolin Group. The school band became so popular for local fundraising activities that the Musicians Protective Union of Grand Junction complained to the commissioner of Indian Affairs about losing business because of the free performances. Museum of Western Colorado.

Teller Institute football team. The boys also played basketball and baseball games against other teams in the league from the local schools. They won their fair share of games. Museum of Western Colorado.

Sledding on the hill overlooking the Southern Ute Boarding School, c. 1910. Museum of Western Colorado.

see a group of children so happy and contented and so well nour-
ished and in such good physical condition as those of the Southern
Ute Boarding School." There were 28 boys and 23 girls in attendance in 1916. They were very proud of the pullman towel system
in use. "The bed linen is changed once a week, aired every day, and
sunned once a week. Toothbrush drill is held twice a day. Eyes are
treated twice a day with Argyrol [an antiseptic], and twice a week
with copper sulphate [to combat trachoma that practically all of the
children suffered from]. Military and exercise drills were to be
started."

Most of the Southern Ute children were attending public schools
in 1916. By 1920, the boarding school was closed and the building
was being used by the Ignacio public school system for all the chil-

Ute children at White Rocks Boarding School, c. 1900. L.C. Thorne collection,
Thorne Studio.

dren in the area. According to a report by the Southern Ute superintendent, the children "take their lunches to school, and since a
child is imitative as well as proud, they require their parents to
supply them with lunches that compare favorably with their white
companions. Their clothing and other needs are on a par with the
white children."

The Fort Lewis Indian Training School sponsored small agency
schools after parents refused to send their children to the Fort
Lewis boarding school. Of the sixteen Ute children sent there in
1892, two died and three became blind.

A 1931 inspector was concerned about the effects of the school
system.

> Among the Southern Utes the majority of those under fifty and all
> under forty can at least write their names. All under thirty-five
> have attended school to the third or fourth grades. Among the Ute
> Mountain Utes, few beyond the age of twenty-five can read or
> write, and I only know of one man over forty who can write his
> name. Among the Paiutes, the adult illiteracy is 100 per cent.

*White Rocks, Utah. As school became an accepted part of Ute life, enrollment
increased. In the 1920s and 1930s most Ute children did not finish grade
school and only a few enrolled in high school or college. L.C. Thorne collection,
Thorne Studio.*

Lindquist Report

During the winter of 1931, G.E.E. Lindquist of Lawrence, Kansas, one of twelve members of the United States Board of Indian Commissioners, was sent to the Consolidated Ute Agency by the board to report on the state of the agency located at Ignacio, Colorado. His detailed report gives a vivid picture of Ute lifestyle after fifty years of reservation life. Although it seems that Lindquist had the welfare of the Indians at heart, his focus followed government policy, which was to care for the Indians and to assist them in living more like their white neighbors.

I found three bands, namely: The Southern Utes, 92 families and 360 individuals; Ute Mountain Utes, 76 families and 440 individuals; and the Paiute band, also known as the Allan Canyon band, with 10 families and 42 individuals. All are restricted, ["restricted" meant the Utes were not allowed to leave the reservations without written permission from their agent.]

All the Ute Mountain land is tribal. Three townships of their land extend into New Mexico. There has been discussion regarding the advisability of buying this land for the Navajos and reimbursing the Utes with other lands at some available point within the State. The thought back of this move is to bring the scattered groups closer together and within easier access of the Ignacio Agency.

The Colorado State Indian Commission, created by Colorado Governor William H. Adams in 1927, was opposed to this sale. The chairman of the advisory group, Mrs. C.W. Wiegel, was "opposed to any sale or exchange of land on the theory that certain treaties, promises, agreements, acknowledgments of ownership, etc. will again become mere scraps of paper to be tossed aside when the white man begins to covet that which is the Indians' by every known right." Lindquist recommended "careful consideration by competent and impartial observers before final action is taken."

Lindquist suggested that Indians be put to work on an irrigation project. The project foreman felt that whites trained for the work should be used since it was not an all-Indian project.

Of the original 375 allotments of land given to the Southern Ute, there were 230 left, the balance having been disposed of by sale or trade. The Allen Canyon band near Blanding, Utah, held 26 small allotments.

Indian employment has been a problem since the Indian were placed on reservations, and the problem has not been solved yet. Indian people have not always been eager to do the type of work assigned to them, and at times they were not considered dependable. This led to the general opinion that Indians were "childlike" and therefore not capable of responsibility. This image is far from accurate. Presently many Indian people hold responsible jobs both within the tribes and in the "outside" world. And there are still many jobs paid for with tribal funds that are not given to qualified Indian workers.

By 1931, the chief source of individual income was the sheep industry. Six thousand sheep could be grazed during the summer months on nearby forest reserves at a low lease rate, reported Inspector Lindquist. "The Ute Mountain people do no farming, their land being arid with little or no water. Consequently these folk roam over a vast area with their flocks, living in tents and wickiups." Chief Ignacio reported he had about one hundred sheep that he kept for the wool. When asked what he did with the money from the sale of wool he replied, "I have got a mouth. I buy things to eat."

The United States government controlled all tribal funds in 1931. Income was generated from oil, gas, and grazing leases and from gratuity appropriations (the monies agreed upon in treaties and other agreements) paid by the government. The Bureau of Indian Affairs negotiated leases, and had the final decision about what the funds were used for.

According to the Lindquist Report:

> These Indians receive annuity payments from tribal funds once a year. This year the Southern Utes received $35 while the Ute Mountain Utes received $50 per capita. All Indians receive rations due to a treaty stipulation. It would seem to be the point of wisdom to have this "treaty obligation be changed," certainly as respects the Southern Utes, as they are apparently able to care for themselves.
>
> I recommended that the available funds of the Utes be husbanded with scrupulous care and expended especially for projects having to do with the stabilization of the home and a general economic advance. The need of stabilizing home life is everywhere apparent. Among the Southern Utes there is no lack of houses, but rather the need of inspiring a new spirit into home making.
>
> The women, as well as the men, are inveterate gamblers. The former largely because they have very few outside, or inside, interests. The gambling among the men has decreased somewhat in recent years, especially since they have sheep to care for and other things to look after on their farms.
>
> Local authorities testify there is no race prejudice between Indians, whites, or Mexicans. However, there is no intermarriage be-

tween Indians and whites although this does occur among the
Mexicans and to a lesser degree among the negroes.

The surrounding population is at least tolerant of the Indians
and at times helpful. More and more white folk in this section of
the country are beginning to realize that the Indian people must
become part and parcel of the general citizenry; that one can not
very well push an Indian into the pit without being carried along
with him, for as the strength of a chain is measured by its weakest
link so is the strength of a community to be gauged by its hum-
blest citizen.

It is interesting to note that there are neither jails nor police
courts in this jurisdiction. Crimes and misdemeanors are handled
by the civil courts. The use of intoxicants, gambling, and promiscuous sexual intercourse are the chief vices. The state of morals is
on a low plane, especially on the Ute Mountain Reservation.

The superintendent put it this way: "A number of the Indians
are married legally while others still practice 'Indian custom' mar-
riages. I can not see any difference; when they get mad at each
other they leave their camp and go to another one. This past year
we have been putting on a special campaign to deal with this situation and I can see some improvement. We have only two Indian
dances each year: in the Spring there is the Bear Dance and in the

*Navajo Springs Subagency was established in 1896 for Chief Ignacio's band of
Weeminuches after they moved en masse in 1895 to the western end of the reservation after refusing to accept the government's policy of allotting land. Their end of
the reservation was retained as land-in-common; eventually separated from the
Southern Ute Reservation as the Ute Mountain Reservation. The agency was
moved to Towaoc in 1917.* Chas. Goodman photo, Colorado Historical Society.

Fall the Sun Dance. The former lasts three days and the latter four."

These Indians have never voted. Colorado has no law against this franchise by Indian citizens. I recommend that steps be taken to instruct and encourage these Utes to vote, thus stimulating their interest in government and inculcating lessons of patriotism.

Ute Mountain Ute Reservation

The Weeminuche band is based on the Ute Mountain Reservation, with headquarters at Towaoc, Colorado. They hold approximately 555,000 acres of land, and have their own tribal government.

In 1895, Chief Ignacio led most of the Weeminuche to the western part of the Southern Ute Reservation in protest against the government's policy of land allotment. Due to the efforts of Chief Ignacio, the Ute Mountain Ute Reservation is now a single piece of communally owned tribal land.

According to the 1931 Lindquist Report:

At Towaoc there is a boarding school, hospital, and subagency located about 100 miles west of Ignacio. The staff at the school number 21, hospital 4, and the subagency 6. This includes a stockman and policeman assigned to the Allan Canyon band. There is need for a community building at Towaoc. The water situation is acute at Towaoc. Apparently it has always been in an acute stage. The well dug at great expense within the past year has not fulfilled expectations.

The first "day school" at Navajo Springs Agency on the Ute Mountain Reservation. Smaller schools located on the reservations had better attendance than the boarding schools far from home. S.F. Stacher, on left, was teacher and his wife was housekeeper. Colorado Historical Society.

♦ Chapter 7
♦ Today's Utes

The Ute people have developed tourism, industry, agriculture, mining, water and gas leases, as well as other ways for earning tribal and individual income. Their tribal offices are modern, efficient, and well run. Schooling that seemed to have no place in Ute life when first introduced has become very important. The *Deseret News* reported, "College for the former generation was almost an impossibility . . . Today not only is it possible but probable." The Ute people have retained their sense of humor, their patience, and their pride. They have never given up their resistance to the lifestyle forced upon them and the loss of what they consider their lands. Since 1897, when they first hired two lawyers to sue for long overdue payments for their lands, they have been fighting a new style of warfare. They have some Indian lawyers now. The fight is still on, using white man's rules in the courtroom.

The Southern Ute tribe opened the Pino Nuche Pu-ra-sa Tourist and Community Center in 1972, offering a modern motel complete with meeting and banquet rooms, restaurant, museum, and arts and crafts shop, as well as the tribal office buildings and recreation areas for the community. The tribe offers guide services during hunting season, access to fishing and camping at Navajo Reservoir, and other services. For information, write to: Southern Ute Tourist Center, Box 282, Ignacio, Colorado 81137.

The Ute Mountain tribe operates a modern pottery shop and showroom. Handcrafted pottery is made here and sold nationwide. The Ute Mountain Tribal Park is being developed as a year-round park where visitors can hike to dwellings of the ancient people, the Anasazi, or take Indian-guided hikes into the backcountry. Tours are arranged by appointment by writing to: Ute Mountain Tribal Park, General Delivery, Towaoc, Colorado 81334.

The Uintah-Ouray Tribe completed its luxurious multimillion-dollar Bottle Hollow Inn and Conference Center in 1976, which offers everything from fine dining to swimming, tennis, fishing, or a visit to the Tribal Museum in one of the unusual concrete tepees. For information, write to: Bottle Hollow Inn, P.O. Box 90, Fort Duchesne, Utah, 84026.

Peyote and the Native American Church

In 1923, Superintendent E.E. McKean at the Consolidated Ute Agency appointed a deputy sheriff to stamp out liquor and drug traffic among the Utes on his reservation. The sheriff's staff raided a group of Utes gathered to use peyote. Their search "yielded up about fifty-five pieces of peyote, along with a small drum said to contain four more pieces." Harry Richard, who seemed to be acting as leader, revealed that he had received a shipment of four hundred pieces about ten days earlier, shipped by parcel post from Henry White in Merriman, Nebraska. McKean wanted to secure a warrant to arrest White on charges of shipping drugs through the mails. He did not want to prosecute the Indians on the reservation. "I can stop their use of peyote without severe punishment," he wrote.

Many Indians opposed the use of peyote. Jim Atwine, a Ute living at White Rocks, Utah, wrote to Washington in 1918 to stop the use of peyote. "This stuff kill so many of my relations," he wrote. "My Uncle Uppa (George To-one-ter), my friend Long Hare, and my brother Charley Sueech have died from eating the bad stuff called peyote."

In 1924, fifty Indians from the Uintah-Ouray reservation petitioned the Department of Interior, United States Indian Field Service, to have the traffic in peyote abolished. The fifty men who signed the petition with their thumbprints next to their written name were most of the old chiefs. They believed "that the use and spread of peyote is very injurious to the Indians who use it, and is the primary cause of death to many of them, and that the use of it destroys their usefulness and ambition, making them lazy and incompetent to do their work." F. Myers, M.D., had written the petition for the Indians and enclosed with it a letter in which he stated that five or six Indians under his care had died from the effects of using peyote, and noted that "the majority of these were young Indians, who could have lived for years. In other parts of the Reservation they are holding peyote meetings, and using the drug to excess. It has a similar effect as morphine, and if continued will destroy

Bertha Grove lived in a tepee with her grandparents as a child, "A lot of these teachings are from my elders and my grandfather, who was a medicine man and a Sun Dance chief. I was the one who worked with him. Went to meetings with a lot of old people. I was 15 or 16 when I began. My teaching began a long time ago." Elizabeth Alexander photograph.

their lives, and wipe out the only true Americans. Stop this traffic before it destroys our Indians," Myers pleaded.

In 1925, the superintendent at the Uintah-Ouray Reservation wrote Washington about his concerns for the considerable membership in the Peyote Church. Since some of the leading members of the church were also very active in the industrial program he decided to "let the matter drift and observe its operation."

Today the Native American Church is a strong influence in the lives of many Native Americans. Because of troubles with the legality of carrying or transporting peyote, Native Americans in many states have chartered their Native American Ceremonies as a legal church.

Ute elder Bertha Grove has been a member of the Native American Church since she was a young woman. She explained she would like people to understand that their religion is a way of life for Indian people. "Many decendants of those whose signatures appear against peyote in that 1924 letter are now leaders in the church," says Bertha.

"We have ceremonies lasting all night (called meetings) for weddings, sickness, birthdays, anniversaries—just like any church. When people are in trouble or have problems, to help them overcome the obstacles, people will pray for them to come through their trouble. It is like an all-night prayer service. You learn a lot in there. For example, the sermons will tell you what the old people would teach, how you are supposed to act in life on the basis of the four things that are in the charter (of the church): love, hope, faith, and charity.

"We are told you cannot abuse (peyote). It is used as a sacrament only through church ceremonies, not in the homes or other times. I would be scared to take it at home. You have to be together (at a meeting) where you can observe what is happening to everyone. We are very strict about that part. It would be terrible to get addicted to. But you don't get addicted, we don't use it like that. We use it for prayer and meditation. Like wine, it is our sacrament. We could probably do without it but it is our sacrament as long as we don't abuse it. Peyote is our way of communicating with the Creator.

"This is God's ceremony. This is the way the doctoring ceremony has been been passed on to us too. The way they told us is, you're the Creator and I'm here and there is the sick person. The sick person is asking for help. Since we are humans, we can only go so far and then it's between the sick person and the Creator. The sick person has to believe. What I've done between the Creator is as far as I can go. It comes full circle. If you are going to doubt what you asked for, you won't get it.

"By his grace am I still alive today, by his grace you can be well but you have to believe in him (the Creator). I know what I'm talking about because that's the way we live. For many people its like a weekend deal, but if you are going to live it the way the old people told us—like Buckskin Charlie and Issac Cloud taught us a long time ago—it's our daily life. It's a *way* of life not a Sunday deal. You live it every day of your life and that's the way I live. I learn to accept what the Creator wants me to do. Building of your own faith and say 'Grandfather take care of this for me.' The Creator says, 'Here she is again, praying about it and when she quits asking then I can do something about her.'

"If you think about it, the white people came here and wanted to get us off the earth. Now the circle has come around and they want to be part of the ceremony. 'You Indians have something we lost or never had. What is it that you have? We want to be a part of that.' Remember, we were the pagans—the savages. What are you people doing here? We kind of turned the tables on you, didn't we?

"There are things we don't talk about and things we don't say because that's the way we are. (Meetings are held in a tepee put up for the meeting and taken down immediately after.) Some people see the tepee come up they say oh, here they go again causing trouble. We are praying even for those who don't understand, we are praying for the four directions and the four races of people.

"We sit up all night long. A traditional Indian is not playing an Indian. We sit in a sweat lodge anytime we are asked to help. Here we are in a sweat lodge three or four times a week standing by someone who needs support—standing the heat and sweating to help ask in supplication, and there we are sitting up all night, singing all night, saying our prayers, getting cramps, sweating, with hurting backs, thirsty, too cold, people crying—bringing all the problems into there and trying to put all our efforts into helping people be well. People don't realize what we go though. Here comes the Sun Dance, here we are again—fasting. Someone calls up in the middle of the night, and here we are again, helping them. We are standing by to help with their problems. There are all kinds of different ceremonies that we go through, different kinds of things that we have. That's our life. That's our life work.

"There is much of the Native American Church that people don't understand. If you are really interested, you come and see for yourself. No person is better than the other one. If you are the president or the poorest, educated, or uneducated, best dressed or not, it doesn't make any difference. God looks at you in his heart. God knows who you are. When the sun comes up it doesn't say, 'I'm not going to shine on you because you're white or black.' Does the rain discriminate? Water doesn't say 'Don't drink me because you are of a certain race.' Does death come and say 'Don't die because you are Indian or white'? The Creator gives you the gift of life as a gift, you don't buy it. You can spend hundreds of millions of dollars—you still are going to die.

"This is a lifetime education. 'You don't graduate from this one,' said the elders. 'We have many things to do. It's hard to be an Indian.'"

Williamette Thompson was born and raised on the Southern Ute Reservation. The 1990 Business Administration graduate of Fort Lewis College is concerned that all tribal peoples are not taking advantage of opportunities to go to school to expand their horizons. "That's a big concern I have. I want my daughter to take advantage of the opportunity. I don't want her to be idle. I'm proud of what I'm accomplishing."

In the fashion of many Indian people, Williamette often pauses when asked a question. "We stop and think," said explains. "We think who we are talking to because we don't want to offend anyone."

She's not sure if she should be considered traditional. "Maybe part time," says Williamette. "I see tradition is like the language;

Williamette Thompson (b. 1963) was selected as Miss Southern Ute in 1979 and 1981. She is wearing her grandmother's traditional elktooth dress, belt, and hair pipe necklace. Each tribal group selects a young woman to act as the tribe's official representative at Native American and other functions. At the Southern Ute reservation, candidates are judged on their knowledge of traditions, the quality and accuracy of their outfit, and their presence. Photo courtesy of Williamette Thompson.

it's not a major part of the younger generation's lives. I can speak some Ute words and understand what people say. My daughter speaks some of the words Grandpa and I teach her. I honor Sun Dance time by honoring my father's wishes as a Sun Dancer. I'm not allowed to do certain things. My dad says *because* I'm a Sun Dancer you're not allowed to use a sharp knife over the stove. As he's Sun Dancing the whole family does not use sharp objects, (only) man made. While getting him ready we use no scissors. We cut things with our teeth.

"I go to Catholic Church and am concerned with Peyote meetings. I tend not to call it Native American Church. To me it's not like a church, it is a place of worship. To me it's like taking communion to go and pray. The first time I took communion I felt this presence like God was really listening and as I take Peyote he is right there. It's like I have his attention. While you're taking Peyote your mind has to be on one focus depending on the purpose of the meeting. Christ is the messenger for God. I pray to him, but as in all things I tend to go to the top.

"I don't feel resentment about living on a reservation," she states. "It's sad that we got such a small portion of the territory the Indians once had. Spiritually nobody owns the land but physically we were forced to claim land to live. Now we have to deal with the reality of contemporary man. The tribe has to be seen as a corporation within the tribal membership. Tribal people need to see the tribe as a governmental corporation. I can see the relationship of the tribe with a big corporation. Per Capita is just the beginning of dividends like a corporation would pay."

Williamette joins many other Utes in the opinion that the tribe should buy back all the undeveloped land within the reservation boundaries. She feels the tribe would prosper from ownership of all the natural resources on this land. "We want to be a nation separated. There are a lot of benefits to being a sovereign nation. There is too much government intervention now. This would be at a minimum if we were separated. We have our separate government now. It's a different life. We deal only with the federal government. Not state or local, although we do deal locally at times when getting license plates and driver's licenses."

Williamette is leaving the reservation for a job in her career field. "I'm doing this for me," she says. "I look forward to the new experience. I feel the best way to help my people is to learn all I can outside my tribe and to bring my help back to my people. When I think I've learned enough I'd like to come back and help. We need all the help we can get! Even if I don't go back, I'd still be part of the growth and long term survival. I'm concerned about my people."

Luke Duncan was born and raised on the Uintah-Ouray Reservation. He left the reservation to go to school at the Institute of American Indian Arts and then to work for Mountain Bell. He left a good job with Mountain Bell to run on the winning ticket of 1989 for the tribal council. "It's good fighting for the rights of your people. I feel that it's something that came along, something that I have to do for everything that I have gained and accomplished in my life. It's my time maybe to give something to my tribe, try to help the situation out somehow. After four years I'd like to go back to my job. I'd really like to go back. That's what I'm going to do. You don't think this type of work is something that a guy would want to take as a lifetime career. This work gets to be hectic sometimes. It's not a glamorous job, I'll tell you that right now. There was a time at work when I used to listen to the radio, and that's as close as I ever came to politics, it was somebody else's problem. Somebody else had to make that decision, now it's right in front of you, and you have to decide what you are going to do.

Luke Duncan, chairman Northern Ute Indian tribe. Jan Pettit photo, 1989.

"I don't have time to just sit here and daydream. Always something going, always something moving. One day we're over in Salt Lake City negotiating for the water and the next day I'm over here talking to the children. You know, to me, I don't see anything more important than the other. They are all important, they're all big issues.

"We're trying to set up a code of ethics for the tribal council. The tribe has a personnel manual that they work under, but yet the tribal council doesn't have anything to regulate our activities. I feel with a code of ethics we'd be accountable for something. Now we're not. Council can come and go as they please and what kind of role model is that? We have guidelines, we need to be in here every day to show them that we're here. I don't want to be one of those people to go against the oath I took into office to uphold the constitution.

"I can tell you what I hope for, that is unity. I'd like to see people helping one another. Maybe somehow we can break that, what shall I say, that little power struggle that we have going on within all reservations. Maybe people can come together and realize it's for the benefit of the tribe as a whole. Rather than one individual here or one family over here.

"Encourage their children and their grandchildren to go on to higher education, so that we can get leaders which are the children now. Maybe by then we'll have our own attorneys and our own doctors that can come back and work for the people here. We can have strong people who know the rights of our people and can work in that direction—for the tribe. Too many times we've seen people come in and work for themselves and I don't like to see that.

When asked about the tale told by some of the elders that says when the Indians are gone the world will be gone, Chairman Duncan replied, "Well, there's a lot of things that go with that. One of the things is the drum, as far as I'm concerned. The drum is the heartbeat of the tribe and as long as we have the drumbeat on the reservations and young boys singing, which we're seeing on our reservation now. Once you let the drum die on your reservation, your tribe is going to die.

"I started singing twenty-some odd years ago. We'd go to a pow-wow and there was a drum sitting there with old guys singing, beating the drum, you could hardly hear them singing. We came along, we were just young guys then, we did something that no other guys had done. We got together and put a group together. And now here we are, we're getting older now, and we're doing one thing that was never done for us. We're supporting the young kids. Our young men at the pow-wows are singing and dancing and that's a step forward and that's just within the last fifteen and twenty years. You go to our pow-wow here, there's many, many dancers. I was proud to see so many of our kids dancing in competition and to hear their last names and to see they are part of us. Hey, that makes a guy feel good.

"We have to play a part in it, a big role. And the children seeing that their parents care and want them to live that way I think it's going to succeed. I hope so, because once that thing is gone—regardless of how much education our people have, you know, the reservation is gone. The Indian people are gone. I'd like to see Indians here forever."

Famous Names and Familiar Places

Utah, Colorado, New Mexico, and Arizona have many streets, parks, mountains, and towns named for the Ute people.

Andrew Frank, left. C.C. McBride photographer, Smithsonian Institution. Inset photo, National Archives.

Andrew Frank (Uintah Band, b. 1878) Frank was a young man well on his way to becoming a leader when he accompanied Red Cap to South Dakota to protest allotment. He was to live long enough hold the honor of being one of the last traditional leaders of the Uintah Band.

Antero, Uintah Ute War Chief.
John K. Hillers photo, Powell Expedition, Smithsonian Institution.

Chief Buckskin Charlie. Smithsonian Institution.

Antero (Graceful Walker) War Chief of the Uintah Utes visited by Major John Wesley Powell in 1873. Antero Reservoir, Antero Junction, Antero Mountain, and other Colorado and Utah sites bear this famous chief's name.

Buckskin Charlie (Moache Band, d. 1936) Great war chief and leader of the Southern Utes. As Ouray lay on his deathbed, he asked Buckskin Charlie to stay with the people and help them through the difficult times they were facing.

Chipeta, wife of Ouray. Photo c. 1907 at Uintah-Ouray Reservation. Smithsonian Institution.

Chipeta (Tabeguache Band, b. 1843, d. 1924) Beautiful, intelligent, and friendly, Chipeta married Chief Ouray in 1859. She held a place of honor among whites and Indians alike. Over five thousand people attended her burial at Chipeta Memorial Monument near Montrose, Colorado.

Cochetope Ute word meaning "pass of the buffalo."

Colorow (White River Band) Chief of the northern Utes, renowned for his wandering and persistent antagonism toward all settlers in Ute country. One of his relatives has this to say about him: "He was moved from Meeker up here to Utah. I don't blame him for being

thing there was to know about operating the heavy photo-
phic equipment he carried for the "professional photographers."
fore long he was appointed official photographer for the many
well expeditions exploring the canyons, valleys, and streams of
lorado, Utah, Arizona, and New Mexico. He was the first to pho-
raph the Grand Canyon. His ethnographic photographs are con-
ered a national treasure.

nacio (Weeminuche Band, b. 1828, d. 1913) Chief and forceful
der who was instrumental in moving his band to the Ute Moun-
n Ute Reservation, where the lands have remained united.

Ignacio. Photo c. 1904. Smithsonian Institution.

bad. He was mad about what was happening to hi
said mean words, and people were afraid of him.
was good to protect his people." Colorow signed trea
1868.

*Curacan
treaty
Washing
well-wor
most lik
from one
cessful ca
the Arap
Kiowa,*
Smithson

e
g
I
I
(

Conejo son of Sabeta, Chief of Capotes.

Curacante (Uncompahgre Band) Curecanti Recreati
near Gunnison, Colorado, was named for this War Chief
ticipated in treaty negotiations in Washington in 1868 an
1873.

Hillers, John K. German emigrant hired as a boat
handyman by John Wesley Powell in 1871. Hillers soon le

Kanoshe (Pauvant Band) Chief hired by Brigham Young to recover the property and body of Captain John W. Gunnison after he had been killed in 1854.

Ouray (Uncompahgre Band, born in 1833, died in 1880) Leader, spokesman and peacemaker for the Ute people. President William McKinley stated, "He was the most intelligent Indian I ever conversed with." According to the western artist, Charles Craig, "He was a wonderful Indian and was one of the finest men I have ever known. A natural leader of his people, big physically and mentally, fair in his dealing with the whites and thoughtful for the best interest of his tribesmen." His portrait holds a place of honor among other famous Colorado pioneers in the dome of Colorado State Capitol.

Pagosa Ute word meaning "Healing water" or "Beaver."

Pahvant Ute word meaning "Close to water."

Powell, John Wesley (b. 1834, d. 1902) In 1868, Powell spent the winter with Ute leaders Antero and Douglas in the White River Valley of Colorado. Between trips to draw maps and make geographical notes, he pursued ethnological studies, learning to speak Ute and recording tales and legends related by elders at long campfire sessions. He was later instrumental in the formation of the American Bureau of Ethnology and served as the director of that Bureau.

Saguache Ute word meaning "Blue Earth" or "Water at the Blue Earth."

Sanpete Ute band in Utah led by Pinasia when Powell visited them in 1872.

Sapinero (Tabeguache Band) Chipeta's brother. He attempted to assassinate Ouray following the signing of a controversial treaty. In later years, he was Ouray's friend.

Severo (Capota Band) Chief and Reservation policeman.

Sevier Paiute word meaning "bison."

Shavano (Tabeguache Band) The name means "Blue Flower."

Ouray. Photo c. 1868. Smithsonian Institution.

Severo and family. Left to right: Capiton, Piah (Peter Snow), Severo (Aaron Bear), Natz-chi-ve-rat, Isareta. c. 1894. H.S. Poley photographer, Smithsonian Institution.

Medicine man and chief who was killed in front of a store at Ouray, Utah, in 1886.

Tabby-To-Kwana (Child of the Sun) Uintah Ute leader who led the starving Utes to the Uintah Basin Reservation in 1869.

Tabeguache Ute word meaning "people who live on the warm side of the mountain."

Tabernash (White River Band) Shot in 1879 after a feud with ranchers.

Tawats ("sun") Better known as Chief Tabby of the Tabeguache Band in 1874.

Tierra Blanca (Moache Band) Leader of Christmas raid on El Pueblo. Easily recognized by a red wool shirt he liked to wear.

Timpanogos Escalante named a mountain Sierra Blanca de los Timpanosis after the Timpanogotzis Indians in that area.

Towaoc Ute word meaning "all right."

Uintah From Ute word *uintaugump*, meaning "at the edge of the pine." Name used for Ute band in Utah.

Uncompahgre From Ute word *ankapagarits*, meaning "red lake." Name used for Ute band in Colorado.

Utah From Ute name *yutas*, meaning "the people."

Ute same as above.

Yampa From the Ute word *yamparika* meaning yampa or carrot eaters. Refers to the tubers of the yampa plant that resemble small sweet potatoes. The band called the Yamparika occupied the area of the Yampa River valley in northeastern Colorado. They were later known as the White River Utes.

Bibliography

Andrews, Ralph W. *Photographers of the Frontier West*. Seattle; Superior Publishing Co., 1965.

Bahti, Tom. *Southwest Indian Tribes*. Flagstaff: KC Publications, 1968.

Bailey, Paul. *Walkara, Hawk of the Mountains*. Los Angeles: Westernlore Press, 1954.

Baker, Augusta. "The Ute Indians." M.A. Thesis, University of Denver, 1926.

Black, Robert C. *Island in the Rockies*: Boulder. Pruett Publishing Co., 1969.

Bolton, Herbert E. *Pageant in the Wilderness: The Story of the Escalante Expedition to the Interior Basin, 1776*. Salt Lake City: Utah State Historical Society, 1950.

Brown, Evelyn. "East Montrose County Colorado, its early History 1880–1920." Thesis, Mesa College, 1955.

Buckles, William. "The Uncompahgre Complex: Historic Ute Archaeology and Prehistoric Archaeology on the Uncompahgre Plateau." PhD. Dissertation, University of Colorado, 1971.

Burnhan, Paul F. "Settlement Patterns on the Ute Indian Reservations," M.S. Thesis, University of Utah, 1980.

Byrne, Bernard J. *A Frontier Army Surgeon*. Cranford, N.J.: Allen Printing Co., 1935.

Campbell, Rosemae Wells. *From Trappers to Tourists*. Palmer Lake, Colo.: The Filter Press, 1972.

Castleton, Kenneth B., *Petroglyphs & Pictographs*. Utah Museum of Natural History, 1978.

Chapin, Frederick H. *The Land of the Cliffdwellers*. Boston; W.B. Clarke and Company, 1892.

Conard, Howard Louis. *Uncle Dick Wootton*. Chicago: Dibble, 1890.

Covington, James Warren. *Relations Between the Ute Indians and the U.S. Government, 1848–1900*. Norman: University of Oklahoma Press, 1949.

Densmore, Frances. *Northern Ute Music*. Washington, D.C.: Bureau of American Ethnology, 1922.

Delaney, Robert W. *The Southern Ute People*. Phoenix: Indian Tribal Series, 1974.

Duke Oral History Project. Mariott Library, University of Utah.

Dutton, Bertha Pauline. *Indians of American Southwest*. Englewood Cliffs, N.J.: Prentice-Hall, 1975.

Emmitt, R. *The Last War Trail*. Norman: University of Oklahoma Press, 1954.

Ferris, W.A. *Life in the Rocky Mountains*. Denver: The Old West Publishing Company, 1940.

Freeman, Dan A. *Four Years with the Utes*. Waco, Texas: U.M. Morrison, 1962.

Hafen, LeRoy R. *Life in the Far West*. Norman: University of Oklahoma Press, 1951.

Harrington, H.D. *Edible Native Plants of the Rocky Mountains*. Albuquerque: University of New Mexico Press, 1967.

Harrington, John P. *The Phonetic System of the Ute Language*. Boulder: University of Colorado Studies, 1911.

Hill, Edward E. *Guide to American Indians*. Washington, D.C.: National Archives, 1981.

Hill, Edward E. *Records of the Bureau of Indian Affairs*, Vol. 1. Washington, D.C.: National Archives Records Service, 1965.

Howbert, Irving. *The Indians of the Pike's Peak Region*. Glorieta, N.M.: Rio Grande Press, 1970.

Hughes, Donald J. *American Indians in Colorado*. Boulder: Pruett Publishing Company, 1977.

Hurst, C.T. *Colorado's Old Timers*. Gunnison, Colo.: The Colorado Archeological Society, 1946.

Iden, Thomas L. "A History of the Ute Indian Cessions of Colorado." Thesis, Western State College, Gunnison, Colorado, 1929.

Jefferson, James, Robert W. Delaney and Gregory C. Thompson. *The Southern Utes: A Tribal History*. Salt Lake City: University of Utah Printing Service, 1972.

Jocknick, Sidney. *Early Days on Western Slope, 1870–83*. Denver: Carson-Harper Co., 1913.

Jorgensen, Joseph G. *The Sun Dance Religion*. Chicago: University of Chicago Press, 1972.

Lang, Gottfried O. A Study in Culture Contact and Culture Change: *The Whiterock Utes in Transition*. Salt Lake City: University of Utah Press, 1953.

Linton, Ralph. *Acculturation in Seven American Indian Tribes*. Gloucester, Mass.: Peter Smith Publishers, 1963.

Lister, Robert H. *Artifacts from the Hauser Site, Montrose, Colorado*. Denver: The Colorado Archeological Society, 1963.

Lyman, June, and Norma Denver. *Ute People: An Historical Study.* Salt Lake City: Uintah School District and the Western History Center, University of Utah, 1969.

Mayfield, Clara M. *The History of the Southern Ute.* New York: Carlton Press, Inc., 1972.

McKern, W.C. *Western Colorado Petroglyphs.* BLM Cultural Resources Series No. 8, 1978.

McClung, Hester. "Diary, 1873." Courtesy of Sue Armitage, Washington State University.

Millich, Arlene A. "Syllabus for Southern Ute Culture and Traditions." 1976 (Unpublished).

National Anthropological Achives, American Ethnology Manuscripts. Museum of Natural History, Washington, D.C.

National Archives of the United States. Colorado Superintendency, Office of Indian Affairs Reports, 1861–1880, Washington, D.C.

National Archives of the United States. New Mexico Superintendency, Office of Indian Affairs Reports, 1824–1880. Washington, D.C.

National Archives of the United States. Utah Superintendency, Office of Indian Affairs Reports, 1849–1880, Washington, D.C.

O'Neil Floyd. *The Reluctant Suzerainty: The Uintah and Ouray Reservation. Utah Historical Quarterly* Pamphlet, 1971.

Porter, Clyde, and Mae Reed. *Ruxton of the Rockies.* Norman: University of Oklahoma Press, 1950.

Pratt, A.G. *Rock Art of the Uintah Basin.* Roosevelt, Utah: Uintah Basin Standard, 1972.

Southern Ute Tribe. *Progress and the Future.* Dallas: Taylor Publishing Company, 1966.

Prucha, Francis Paul. *Indian Peace Medals in American History.* Lincoln: University of Nebraska Press, 1971.

Rippeteau, Bruce Estes. *A Colorado Book of the Dead.* Denver: Colorado Magazine, 1978.

Riddle, Ida Wheaton. "Letters." Colorado College Library.

Rockwell, Wilson. "The Formative Years." Manuscript. Delta Museum Delta, Colo.

Rockwell, Wilson. The Utes: A Forgotten People. Denver: Sage Books, 1956.

Ruxton, George Frederick Augustus. *Wild Life in the Rocky Mountains.* New York: Outing Publishing Co., 1924.

Sabin, E.L. *Kit Carson Days 1809–1868.* New York: The Press of the Pioneers, 1935.

Smith, Anne Milne. *Ethnography of the Northern Utes*. Santa Fe: Museum of New Mexico Press, 1974.

Smith, P. David. *Ouray Chief of the Utes*. Ouray: Colo.: Wayfinder Press, 1986.

Steward, Julian Haynes. *Aboriginal and Historical Groups of the Ute Indians of Utah*: An Analysis with Supplement. New York: Garland Pub., Inc., 1974.

Stewart, Omer C. *Ethnohistorical Bibliography of the Ute Indians of Colorado*. Boulder: University of Colorado Press, 1971.

Stewart, Omer C. *Ethnography of the Eastern Ute*. Boulder: University of Colorado Press, 1977.

Stewart, Omer C. *Ethnography of the Western Ute*. Boulder: University of Colorado, 1973.

Stone, Wilbur F. *History of Colorado*. Chicago: S.J. Clarke Publishing Co., 1918.

Swadesh, Frances Leon. *Los Primeros Pobladores*. Notre Dame: University of Notre Dame Press, 1974.

Terrell, John Upton. *The Man Who Rediscovered America*. New York: Weybright and Talley, Inc., 1969.

Thomas, Alfred Barnaby. *After Coronado: Spanish Exploration of New Mexico, 1696–1727*. Norman, University of Oklahoma Press, 1935.

Thomas, Alfred Barnaby. *Forgotten Frontiers: A Study of Don Juan Baustista de Anza, Governor of New Mexico, 1777–87*. Norman: University of Oklahoma Press, 1932.

Thomas, Alfred Barnaby. *The Plains Indians and New Mexico, 1751–1778: A Collection of Documents Illustrative of the History of the Eastern Frontier of New Mexico*. Albuquerque: University of New Mexico Press, 1940.

Toll, Henry Wolcott. *Delores River Archeology*. BLM Cultural Resources Series No. 4, 1971.

Twitchell, Ralph Emerson. *The Spanish Archives of New Mexico*. Cedar Rapids, Iowa: The Torch Press, 1914.

Tyler, S. Lyman. "Before Escalante: An Early History of the Yuta Indians and the Area North of New Mexico." PhD. Thesis, University of Utah, 1951.

U.S. Dept of Commerce, Bureau of Census. 1970 Subject Reports, American Indians. University of Utah. Issued June 1973.

U.S. 46th Congress, 2nd session, 1879–1880 Senate. "Correspondence Concerning the Ute Indians in Colorado." Washington: U.S. Government Printing Office, 1879.

Index